in
touch
with

2005

dance

marion gough

First Published in 1993 by Whitethorn Books,
Hindburn House, Wray, Lancaster LA2 8QB
Copyright © Marion Gough 1993

ISBN 1 873783 01 9

Designed by Christopher Lord
Dance consultant to Whitethorn Books:
Jane Mooney
Photographer for Ludus Dance Company:
Dee Conway
Photographer for Contemporary Dance Trust:
Adam Eastland
PR Consultant to Whitethorn Books:
Maura Peake, Brainwave PR
Typeset by Vernon Hayes Graphics
Cover photograph George Mooney
Illustrations by Dennis Tinkler
Printed in Great Britain by Shanleys, Bolton

contents

Acknowledgments

My thanks to the late Joan Russell who inspired me to begin in dance education and Marion North who encourages me to continue. To colleagues past and present at the Laban Centre for their friendship and support. Thanks also to those many ex-students, whose creative and imaginative work continues to impress me - particularly Jane, Madalena, Jeff and Louise. Thanks to Amanda, who carries on the tradition - and to Victoria, who doesn't. Many thanks to Bob for his invaluable help and perceptive advice. Thanks to Pete and Chris for all their enthusiasm and commitment.

Finally, thanks to Jane for persuading me to be begin writing - and to Raymond for his vision, time and attention and for supporting this publication so generously.

A note on style

Despite the richness of the English language, there were two particular difficulties for me in writing this book. Firstly, the matter of the personal pronoun. Whilst wishing to avoid the inclusive use of the masculine form, I did not want awkward constructions ('He or she should ensure that her or his ...'). Some education writers use 'she' exclusively - presumably to compensate for years of the reverse. In a book about dance this might well reinforce some of the unfortunate stereotypes which abound. In written form, 's/he' works well and I have mostly used this and otherwise sought appropriate balance without making the text too unwieldy.

The second matter is to do with how we refer to those whom we are teaching. 'Children' is inappropriate, given the age range; 'boys and girls' not entirely satisfactory, 'kids,' awful. 'Pupils' seems somewhat stilted, and yet 'students' won't do either - given the convention that this term seems to be applied to those in further and higher education (although Americans don't have this problem - all from the age of 6 are 'students'). In most cases, therefore, I have settled for 'young people'.

foreword

For most people, dance embodies poignant and evocative memories: losing oneself in dance at a party, the clumsy tenderness of the last slow number at the disco, or perhaps the excitement of giving form to our feelings and thoughts in our own dance composition. Dance is intimately connected with feeling, with our emotional life, and like other performed arts it demands openness, commitment and honesty. Anything less compromises the directness of communication which is the hallmark of dance at its best.

For the professional performer, dance can be almost brutal - fiercely demanding of the body, mind and spirit. Yet dancing is often thought of as frivolous or shallow, a marginal pursuit, an esoteric art form on the fringes of education for the 'real world'. Dancers and dance teachers know differently. They are aware of the concentration, the attention to detail, the rigour and sheer hard work which go into making an 'effortless' performance. Those who work in the studio (or hall or gym) are familiar with a process of creation which engages the whole person as few other art forms do.

Dance is not better than music, drama or art, but like each of them it is uniquely **itself.** Untranslatable, it exists in the moment of its making. Ephemeral, it demands to be experienced at first hand - whether as a dancer or as a spectator at a live performance. Dance is inscribed on the body and so always relates to our experience of what it is to be human. At the same time it is rarely literal, but instead engages the watcher actively in making meaning as much as in deciphering it. Its metaphorical richness can make it challenging, but for many young people it is an eloquent expression of the immediacy of their own experience of the physical world.

Dance in schools is no less demanding and no less rewarding than dance in the theatre. For the professional dance artist, working with young people in the school context is an opportunity to share insights and to experience - often as if for the first time - the liberating and creative power of dance, and its life-affirming force. In her teaching, and in this book, Marion Gough places dance squarely in the context of the other arts and of the world around us. She clearly articulates a view of the dance lesson as a dynamic process in which teacher and young people actively engage in learning, discovering and making dance together, always pursuing refinement and precision in physical expression. In this approach we see reflected our own pursuit of excellence, of quality - in two senses: both the palpable texture of physical experience and the power of effective artistic expression.

Throughout this book is an unwavering commitment to empowering the dance teacher, for it is only through the continuing professional development of the teacher that the entitlement of young people to artistic expression in dance will be fully realised.

If, though you have picked up this book, you are hesitant about teaching dance or unsure of your feelings about it, may we offer a simple prescription: put on a record and dance in the front room; watch the video of "Strictly Ballroom"; go to see some live dance - contemporary, South Asian, ballet, African, Irish; join a dance class or club - in short do whatever you need to do in order to renew your personal contact with the experience of dancing. Then read and use this book to help you transform the gym or school hall into a place of excitement and discovery.

Christopher Thomson, Director, Education and Community Programmes
Contemporary Dance Trust

Pete Johnson, Education Officer
Ludus Dance Company

September 1993

introduction

As you open this book, and leaf through its pages, sections and chapters, you will want to be sure that it can lead you to new ground in your understanding and experience of dance. That, precisely, is its intention.

The text moves towards a clear destination - starting out from familiar territory, from what you may know already - revisiting, refreshing and securing the essential starting points of understanding, then continuing onward to explore and reveal the unusual, the surprising, the new ways of working that produce QUALITY in the dance progress of young people. Surely it is not enough just to 'get children moving', to fulfil the minimum obligations of a pre-set curriculum or schedule of lesson activities.

Learning to dance involves young people in discovery and progression - and in doing so to experience joy, elation and real achievement. As a teacher you may want to know more about how to develop and manage such a process. If so, then this book is for you. It is written for those willing to go beyond the basics, wishing to pursue excellence.

More people participate in dancing than in acting, writing, painting, singing or playing music. In spite of this, dance is all too rarely included in discussion about the arts - even amongst educationalists, critics and other arts practitioners.

It is not surprising, therefore, to find that dance in education is not highly valued. The Cinderella status of dance as a curriculum subject is due in part to:

- its history being a relatively short one, with little tradition on which to draw

- the ephemeral and transitory nature of the activity; once it is over it leaves no visible traces

- it is still in the main seen as a subject for girls, taught by women

- it is not seen as a subject in its own right, but as one of a number of physical education activities

Dance is often the least well resourced subject in terms of staffing, space, equipment and books. Dance teachers have constantly to fight against ill-conceived ideas about the subject. It is frequently undervalued both by teachers and parents, who might well be unfamiliar with dance in education and their perception of the subject consequently limited and prejudiced.

As a consequence, teaching dance today can be very demanding; the dance teacher often feels isolated because s/he may well be the only dance teacher in the school and have very little opportunity for in-service support and provision. It is not necessary that the teacher be a dancer, but s/he should know what it feels like to dance and should have experienced dancing. The good teacher will act as initiator, guide, observer, enthuser, evaluator and critic.

How can we, as teachers, promote interest and positive attitudes towards dance? How can we encourage young people, male and female, to have a positive body image and develop self-confidence? How can we stimulate their imagination and creativity? How can we make dance relevant and contribute to the world we live in?

This book confronts the difficulties and gives consideration to such questions. It is for students and teachers, both new and experienced, who may wish to consider different approaches. It is intended for teachers of the middle years and will be particularly significant for Key Stages 2 and 3 of the National Curriculum, in that it will encourage continuity and progression. The book aims to support teachers by exploring an extensive range of ideas for dance; it provides a framework for developing a dance curriculum as well as suggestions about methods, resources and materials readily adaptable to the varying developmental needs of young people in this age range.

It draws attention to resources for dance and makes links with other art forms. It promotes the idea and practice of the teacher as 'partner' with other professional artists - and places the learning and development of young people at the centre of an educational, artistic and aesthetic process. In every section it highlights the 'keys to quality' - ideas and activities that will assist you in enabling young people to move beyond the cliché, the mundane and the predictable.

Dancing enables us to be comfortable in and with our own bodies. Dance, through its expressive and communicative qualities, allows us to become more conscious of ourselves and the world around us in a unique way.

"Dance is one of the few human activities in which the individual is totally involved, body, soul and mind." Maurice Bejart *(Garaudy 1973)*

Marion Gough, September 1993

chapter
one

beginning: first principles

Why Dance in the Curriculum?

It seems customary these days to re-examine the content and methods of the education of young people and redesign them at increasingly frequent intervals. Whilst there are the obvious dangers of continual instability in this process, there may be even more danger in not asking any questions at all.

For many adults a lack of physical confidence or a vague awareness of awkwardness or ill-directed energy may reflect a lack of a balanced educational experience in childhood and adolescence. Dance may not yet be established as an essential experience throughout the totality of a child's education, but there is a growing recognition of its potential to integrate physical, emotional and intellectual development:

"Dance makes a distinctive contribution to the education of all pupils, in that it uses the most fundamental mode of human expression - movement. Through its use of non-verbal communication pupils are able to participate in a way which differs from any other area of learning. It provides aesthetic and cultural education, opportunities for personal expression and it also introduces students to a wealth of traditional, social and theatrical forms. In a broad and balanced curriculum this important area of human experience should not be neglected." CDET/NATFHE/NDTA/SCODHE *(1989)*

All young people should have the opportunity to encounter and to become familiar with this unique form of artistic expression. This book is concerned with how this might happen in schools.

Dance lessons help young people to:

- use their bodies skilfully and creatively
- develop their creativity and imagination
- use expressive movement as a means of communication
- encourage an awareness of others and sensitivity towards them
- analyse form and quality in movement
- derive aesthetic understanding through the creation of dance and the appreciation of dance works
- extend their musical education
- stimulate and heighten work in other areas of the curriculum

How may teachers be successful in fostering these aims? Consistent with any other aspects of education, the teaching of dance is founded on well tested principles and techniques. As a teacher, you will want to be equipped with adequate and appropriate means to develop material for dance. Movement is the medium of expression for dance. Methods of movement analysis, derived from Laban's body of knowledge, give teachers a wide vocabulary from which they can select suitable material for their dance classes, refine and develop young people's movement ability and critically observe their responses and needs.

Clearly implied is:

- the need for a clear understanding of a **body of knowledge and skills**

- the need to place that body of knowledge and skills in a **structure for each lesson**, and

- the need to prepare a **safe and supportive environment**

Let us take each of these in turn.

Body of Knowledge and Skills

The first step is to specify clearly the intention of the lesson:

- Decide on its **movement aims**

Then when preparing material, consider the following:

- **What** movements do we do?

- **Where** do we move?

- **How** do we move?

- With **whom (or what)** do we move?

The following diagram develops these questions and offers a possible framework from which to select movement material for the dance class. Teachers will need to provide a wide range of movement experiences for their young people to ensure a balanced curriculum. When planning a lesson, the movement aim and intention should be paramount.

Movement Aims

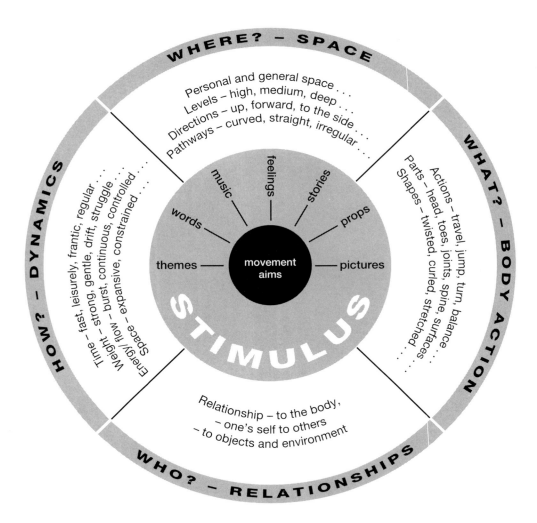

WHERE? – SPACE

Personal and general space . . .
Levels – high, medium, deep . . .
Directions – up, forward, to the side . . .
Pathways – curved, straight, irregular . . . .

WHAT? – BODY ACTION

Actions – travel, jump, turn, balance . . .
Parts – head, toes, joints, spine, surface . . .
Shapes – twisted, curled, stretched . . . .

HOW? – DYNAMICS

Time – fast, leisurely, frantic, regular . . .
Weight – strong, gentle, drift, struggle . . .
Energy/ flow – burst, continuous, controlled . . .
Space – expansive, constrained . . . .

WHO? – RELATIONSHIPS

Relationship – to the body,
– one's self to others
– to objects and environment

STIMULUS

music
feelings
stories
words
props
themes — movement aims — pictures

Accompaniment also needs to be considered:
voice, sounds, percussion, music, silence, text.

Movement aims refers to the material which is to be explored and developed. When considering selection of material for the dance lesson, the movement aims should be of primary importance and no other stimulus may be necessary.

> *Example:* Movement Aims - weight and suspension

If a *stimulus* is to be used, it should be considered as a starting point to encourage a dialogue between teacher and young people. Careful selection is necessary to ensure that a stimulus heightens movement awareness, does not become restrictive and does not dominate the dance class.

> *Example:* Movement Aims - travel, turn, gesture
>
> *Stimulus:* A journey - across different terrains
> e.g. water, rock, sand;
>
> - or exploring different landscapes,
> e.g. cave, mountain, lake, car park,
> waste ground, scrap yard

"No matter what the stimulus for the dance may be it is the opportunities for movement and the logical development of that which should determine the course of the lesson."

Rosamund Shreeves *(Ward Lock Educational 1982)*

Movement aims are signposts; they inform and direct our selection of activity in order to systematically build up a broad vocabulary of movement that the young person needs to acquire. In achieving this the teacher will attempt to achieve a balance in four main areas that allow young people to extend their range of movement and increase their technical skills. The teacher will need to take care that her/his own movement preferences do not dominate, or the diet becomes limited. The order in which material is studied needs to be carefully considered to work for logical progression and increased understanding.

When planning a lesson attention has to be given to the following areas:

Body/Action

Space

Dynamics

Relationship

Whilst each of these will play a part, each lesson has its focus and will be more productive if the movement aims are specific. For example, a lesson which explores elements of **weight** and **suspension** will draw mainly from **dynamics** but set that within a more complete movement context using the following guiding questions:

What actions are used?

Is the whole body involved in the action?

How is the space used?

What emphasis is given to changes of time and energy?

Is the dance performed as a solo or with others?

Planning in this way will ensure a clear aim and intention for both young people and teacher and will provide a sharper focus to evaluation of the work.

what?
body/ action

The physicality of the movement

Actions ———— Movement, stillness, travelling jumping, twisting, transferring weight, gesture, bending, stretching, falling, tilting . . . . .

Parts ———— Whole body, head, torso, limbs, surfaces, joints, spine, front, back, side, arms, legs, feet, hands, elbows, knees, hips, shoulders, ankle, wrist, centre, extremities, finger tips, base of spine, nape of neck . . . . .

Shapes ———— Stretched, curved, angular, wide, narrow, twisted, symmetrical, asymmetrical . . . . .

lesson ideas

1. Develop phrases of movement from the following sets of action words:
   walk, jog, dodge, run or
   swing and swing, turn, balance, fall, recover.
   The imagery from a game or sports activity could be introduced when either sequence is established.

2. Devise two movement phrases concentrating first on the upper, and then lower, torso. Try to perform them together. This is particularly challenging in terms of co-ordination.

The Body in Action Photo: Adam Eastland Contemporary Dance Trust

where?

space

The Dance Environment

Personal and General ———————— Close to and away from the body, near to and far away, toward and away from others, use of focus . . . . .

Directions ———————— Up and down, forward and backward, side to side, diagonally . . . . .

Levels ———————— High, medium, low, off, across and into the floor, through the air . . . . .

Pathways ———————— Direct and meandering, linear, straight, curved, zig-zag, angular, roundabout . . . . .

Patterns ———————— Air, floor, body shape, group design . . . . .

lesson ideas

1. Put together a sequence exploring the sculptural concept of the body in space involving a standing, kneeling, sitting, lying design (see Lesson 8).

2. Consider how a variety of different spaces influence the content of a dance. Examples: a church, a railway station, a staircase, a field, a telephone box.

3. Explore the performance space in terms of the effectiveness of a dance in relation to the audience. Consider the most effective use of *directions, pathways and focus.*

Different Spaces Photo: Adam Eastland Contemporary Dance Trust

how?

dynamics

**The Expression and
Artistry of the Movement**

Flow/energy ———————— Smooth, sustained, regular, continuous, sudden, percussive, irregular, bursting, flowing, explosive, contained, fluent, slow, fast, controlled, erratic . . . . .

Weight ———————— Firm, strong, heavy, powerful, fine, delicate, light, gentle . . . . .

Space ———————— Direct, flexible, linear, meandering . . . . .

Time ———————— Quick, hasty, hurried, fast, slow, leisurely, prolonged, rhythmic, impulsive, impactive, increasing, decreasing, sudden, gradually changing . . . . .

lesson ideas

1. Devise a short movement sequence. Observe the dynamic changes when trying it:
    to different kinds of music, e.g. lyric, rhythmic;
    when using imagery of different colours to influence the quality of movement, for example, red, blue, green, yellow (see Lesson 7).

2. Explore movement suggested by the following words:
    flowing, delicate, leisurely, erratic, impactive, percussive.
    Put together a sequence concentrating on the dynamic qualities of the words.

    Let the order be decided by chance with the throw of a die.

Energy and Motion Ludus Dance Company

Making Connections

Solo ——————— Body parts
Near to, apart from, approaching . . . . .

Duos ——————— Leading, following, facing, mirroring,
side by side . . . . .

Groups ——————— Harmony, opposition; simultaneous,
successive; complementing, con-
trasting; unison, canon . . . . .

Objects and Environments ——————— Cloth, costume, suitcase, newspaper,
driftwood, chairs, ladders, doorways,
corners . . . . .

lesson ideas

1. Devise a solo dance which involves
   the use of associated or random
   objects, e.g. rubber gloves, a step
   ladder, a bucket, a wellington boot **or**
   a book, a can of beans, a biro, a
   sweeping brush.

2. Compose a group dance which uses
   one of the following choreographic
   forms:
   ternary A B A
   theme and variations
   canon and unison

A Structure for Each Lesson

There are many ways to prepare and present dance material. We have already looked at the importance of movement aims and body of knowledge. Progression should be logical and the work should be carefully structured to provide a safe context. It is desirable to establish a balance between:

- activity and relaxation
- exploration and selection and refinement
- participation and observation

The following headings are useful in planning the structure of a lesson. It is a tried and tested approach. This book includes a number of lesson plans which use the following format.

Movement Aims (already considered and related to the potential movement vocabulary)
Introduction/Warm up
Exploration and Development
Appreciation and Evaluation

Introduction/warm up

Warming up is concerned with preparing the body for dance. Young people should be made aware of the effects of exercise on the body. It needs to be thoroughly warm and properly prepared for any strenuous physical activity which may follow. Included should be activities which raise the pulse rate and the body temperature, mobilise joints, warm muscles and strengthen the body. The warm up should include **whole body activities**, such as stretching, bending, swinging and circling as well as work on **individual body parts**. Feet and legs require adequate preparation for what is to follow - jumps, for example. Attention needs to be given to the release of tension, and time allowed for recovery, at the end of a strenuous exercise.

Teachers should ensure that activities are consistent with safe body management. Good alignment, with emphasis on the correct centre of balance when standing, should be emphasised i.e. weight over the balls of the feet. Encouragement should be given to good posture, e.g. standing tall, shoulders down, head high, long neck and arms.

Exercises should build in terms of energy and complexity. Part of the warm up should include travelling, involving simple space awareness and awareness of other members of class. By the end of the warm up the teacher should aim to have established a positive working atmosphere with the class, in which each individual is centred and focused. This requires alertness in mind and body and a readiness to concentrate on what is to follow.

The Body - map

key elements in ensuring a comprehensive approach to warming up

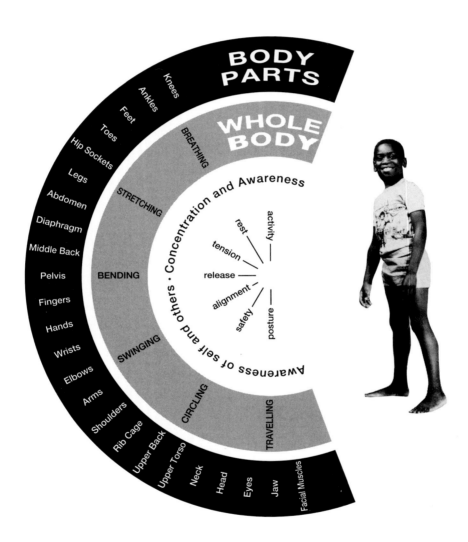

BODY PARTS

Knees
Ankles
Feet
Toes
Hip Sockets
Legs
Abdomen
Diaphragm
Middle Back
Pelvis
Fingers
Hands
Wrists
Elbows
Arms
Shoulders
Rib Cage
Upper Back
Upper Torso
Neck
Head
Eyes
Jaw
Facial Muscles

WHOLE BODY

BREATHING
STRETCHING
BENDING
SWINGING
CIRCLING
TRAVELLING

Concentration and Awareness · Awareness of self and others

activity
rest
tension
release
alignment
safety
posture

Achieving quality means selecting a pattern of activity which:

● builds a whole body consciousness

● warms the body properly

● anticipates future movement activities that will be explored later.

Photo: Chris Harris Ludus Dance Company

The warm up material should reflect the movement aims of the session and lead appropriately to the **Exploration and Development** section. This means that if the lesson, for example, is dealing with space (see Lesson 2), then the movements of the warm up need to connect with or 'anticipate' future skill requirement such as activities travelling in curved pathways. This deepens the movement experience for young people as it places the dance material in a movement context that they can draw from later. It also helps them to identify and make a relationship between the body skills they are developing in the warm up and the application of these in their own movement exploration.

The keys to quality: warm up

a) Start by thinking about what you want to achieve as an outcome from the lesson.

b) Select warm up activities that help prepare the young people with the awareness and skills repertoire that they will need later in the lesson.

c) Try to hold the 'body-map' picture in your head as a means of always achieving an effective balance between the 'part' and the 'whole' in your selection.

d) Remember the objective is to achieve a state of readiness, alertness and concentration - as well as a properly warmed body - so aim to build attentiveness.

e) Avoid tendencies for movement to be careless. Encourage proper 'articulation' in each element, describing and demonstrating the qualitative characteristics of each movement in such a way that the young people are persuaded to 'extend', or 'complete' and so gain an enhanced consciousness of each body part, its potential and participation in the construction of larger movement.

Experiencing Alignment Photo: Adam Eastland Contemporary Dance Trust

Exploration and development

This section is divided into two parts:

1. The first part is concerned with the **exploration of new ideas** arising from the chosen movement aims and with extending young people's vocabulary. It may involve some or all of the following activities:

imitation (copying) ● variation (re-arranging, expanding, contrasting) ● repetition (mastery)

Progression from familiar to unfamiliar movement patterns should be encouraged. Young people should be challenged to consider new possibilities to improve and perfect movements and to find different ways of developing material for dance.

The use of contrast is a helpful way to highlight particular movement characteristics.

> *Examples:* Very quick movements contrasted with a moment of stillness.
> Movement material using the whole body in an expansive way
> is highlighted by a moment of focus on a particular body part.

Adequate time is needed to explore movement experiences in order that young people feel secure when given the task of creating sequences.

2. The second part is concerned with the **development of movement skills** which need to be practised. Young people should be encouraged to select, repeat and clarify their work - on their own or with others - to form dance sequences.

They should work towards a finished dance composition, no matter how short, which they have practised and repeated. If the dances are considered to be of worth, opportunity should be given for them to be observed by members of the class.

The keys to quality: exploration and development

- Help young people innovate by extending familiar movement vocabulary e.g. making a phrase 'very small' or 'very large', embellishing part of it (see Lesson 10) or when combining with a partner, add a travelling section and moments of body contact (see Lesson 8). Often the surprise is in unusual movement combinations or breaking up set patterns.

- Look for the potential. Take something small and by using evocative images allow young people to re-work the same material from many different perspectives.

- Continually seek for ways in which the young people can work through a developing vocabulary of movement systematically, experiencing the effect of refining and transforming through contrast .

Appreciation and evaluation

The showing and observing of dance pieces should be treated seriously. Performers should demonstrate commitment to the work in terms of involvement and preparation and there should be an expectation of high standards. Concentration, on the part of the viewers, is necessary and participation, by observing and commenting on each other's work, should be encouraged. This ought to be led by the teacher with suggestions as to how the class should observe.

> *Examples:* What directions, pathways and levels are used in the travelling sequences? Which body part leads the gesture?
>
> How has the basic motif been developed?
> What needs to happen next?

The keys to quality: evaluation

- Development of accurate observation skills is a key part of the learning process for young people within their overall development. Do not assume that they can see what you see. Their eyes become more trained when you encourage them to describe in detail what they are seeing - prior to making any judgement about it! You can help them focus by directing their attention through questions such as those above.

- Over the period of a curriculum year, effort should be made to build up and periodically reinforce a set of criteria through which young people can learn to evaluate what they are seeing. Clearly they will need help in learning to apply criteria in order to make valid judgements. We will go into this aspect of development in depth at a later stage in this book. References should be made to the Movement Aims - have they been successfully achieved? More detailed reference will be made to this later.

The Need to Prepare a Safe and Supportive Environment

Good planning and preparation give a teacher security. This can enable the experienced teacher to dispense with, or alter, the plan when it is not working or when more productive ideas emerge.

It is important to consider teaching as a two-way process to which both teacher and young people contribute. This requires the teacher to be open-minded and adaptable and gives young people a sense of involvement and responsibility.

How we begin a class is extremely important as it can significantly influence the success or failure of what follows. Particular attention should be given to the mood of the class and this can depend upon:

- **What has taken place before**
  Are they excitable, lethargic, edgy, resentful?

- **The temperature**
  Is it a very hot/bitterly cold day?

- **The conditions**
  Are they to work in an exposed place, used as a thoroughfare, or in a dining room with a dirty floor?

Teachers will need to take account of these kinds of considerations and decide on the most appropriate way to begin.

> *Example:*   A gradual build towards lively, energetic movement for a lethargic group.

The keys to quality: environment

- Whilst the teacher needs to be adaptable, it is not 'precious' to demand a sympathetic working environment in which young dancers can achieve their best.

- For dance to be truly valued it needs to be properly resourced.

chapter two

developing quality: the teacher's strategy

The Development of Quality

Many elements of the approach outlined in the first chapter may be familiar to you. If so, you will recognise that they are pre-conditions for successful work with young people in dance - particularly if that work has to be sustained over long periods of time (such as throughout a school curriculum) and has to produce evidence of satisfactory progress. This will involve giving consideration to such questions as: how can you improve this movement? this sequence? this dance? It also involves examination of the qualitative nature of each task in order to encourage performance to the highest standards.

Everything that follows in this chapter refers back to the foundations established in chapter one. If those foundations are not in place, the practices now recommended may be continually undermined. Most teachers want to see - and measure - progress in the achievement of the young people they work with. Equally, how common (and frustrating) is the experience of never seeming to be able to move far beyond the basics. Teaching then becomes a repetitious cycle, with the unhappy prospect of having to maintain the interest of young people who themselves become very aware when they are not challenged. Perhaps this is your experience also. What can be done ?

Often the solution lies less in the variety of resource material or ideas available to the teacher and more in the way in which the teacher brings her/himself to the task. This chapter examines the ways in which the teacher can develop her/himself - and in doing so be rewarded in the quality of what is achieved with young people.

Eight areas of development are identified as the 'keys' to success for the teacher who wants to take dance to new levels of quality within the day-to-day working context of the school.

The Keys to Quality

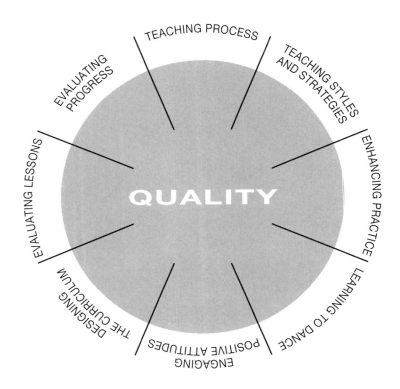

The Teaching Process

Good teaching is concerned with more than knowledge, skills and competencies. It is also about an ability to communicate enthusiasm for the subject and a belief in the right of young people to experience the best possible teaching environment. It requires from the teacher a continuing curiosity regarding the processes of teaching and learning and an openness to considering ways of improving the quality of her/his work.

None of this is new. Teachers concerned about their professional development and improving the quality of their work have always addressed these issues.

However, the constraints of the curriculum, the low status of dance as a subject, the pressure of over-large classes and poor working conditions - particularly as these apply to the teacher of dance - make it more difficult these days to devote time and thought to the processes of exploration and rediscovery of the underlying essence of what dance is all about.

Despite the difficulties of working in such an environment, it remains important for teachers to retain an energy and freshness of approach in order to maintain a perspective about professional growth and development. One aim of this book is to help teachers toward this perspective.

The teacher, especially perhaps in the dance context, constitutes the major resource.

The way in which someone teaches - at any level and in any context - is strongly influenced by a set of personal philosophies, which may be implicit rather than explicit. These philosophies, which inform a teacher's practice, derive from her/his training, background and experience. They also help to constitute a set of values about the process of education. The approach of the teacher will reflect her/his views about the nature of dance knowledge, of teaching and learning and of the needs of young people.

The dance curriculum should be developed in an imaginative and creative way.

> *Examples:* Can tasks be set where the outcomes are not pre-determined and which allow for individuality of expression?
>
> Can dance be presented as an enabling process by which young people take on responsibility for their own development?
>
> Can they be fully challenged to make maximum progress?

Achieving such progression implies a teaching process which provides an invigorating context which encourages young people to develop to their full potential.

Photo: Ludus Dance Company

Teaching Styles and Strategies

Each one of us has a particular way of teaching to which we hold, that reflects our personality, skills and beliefs. Whilst essentially retaining this, one's repertoire should include a variety of styles and strategies to enable young people to learn more effectively and for the work to be of good quality.

Decisions about the most appropriate way of teaching to create an effective learning environment and ensure quality will need to take account of:

a) the subject matter - which teaching style is most appropriate for the task?

b) the young people - will they learn best if taught as an entire class, in groups or as individuals?

During the lesson, one method might predominate or a number of strategies might be used. Quality of outcome will depend on the approach chosen.

Teachers might find the following strategies useful:

1. Demonstration (or 'Do as I do').

The method is didactic - the teacher has the knowledge and skills, and makes all the decisions. S/he has control of the scope, content and pacing of the subject matter which a young person receives. The teacher demonstrates the material which the young person is required to copy as accurately as possible. This approach demands total attention and is particularly relevant when working with very young children. It is especially appropriate when teaching skills or set material; e.g. a warm up phrase, a technique class (Graham) or a dance style (Bharata Natyam). The objectives are clear and the outcome is intended to be the same for everyone.

Demonstration needs to be clear and of good quality. However, this method requires of a young person a facility to translate observed movement into her/his own body. Not everyone finds this easy. Initially you may have to build up young people's ability to RECOGNISE and DESCRIBE accurately what it is they are observing. This is best achieved by questioning what they see, asking them to describe as specifically as possible and encouraging them to differentiate between examples of varying accuracy. Such differentiation sharpens their attentiveness and perceptiveness.

It is usually most helpful to begin by demonstrating a complete sequence fully in the desired movement qualities, as well as use of impulses, accents and tempi, before breaking the material down into smaller sections. This gives a young person an overall impression and an awareness of what to aim for. Teachers should accompany the movement with descriptive vocabulary or imagery to indicate the quality of movement, dynamic changes, etc.

> *Examples:* The movement is initiated by the pelvis.
>
> Weighty, even, swinging movement - imagine a pendulum.
>
> The stretch should extend out beyond the fingertips.

Time should be allowed:
a) to break down material,
b) to give feedback and corrections,
c) to repeat and clarify, where necessary.

When breaking down material into smaller sections be sure that the sense, flow and continuity are not lost. When giving corrections, be selective. Do not give too much information at once. Concentrate on one or two elements until they have been perfected before adding to the task.

Direct physical manipulation can be helpful when correcting an individual to clarify bodily intention. However, be sensitive to gender and to cultural taboos about the use of touch. Time given to young people to repeat and clarify sections of work allows teachers the opportunity to help individuals needing more attention or to add challenges to those who are ready for them.

This approach can also be used with young people's own work. An individual who has produced imaginative material might be asked to teach this for the rest of the class.

2. Self-evaluation.

An example of self-evaluation would be that the young people are given a task, the content of which is set by the teacher and on which they are to work for a set period of time. The content and movement quality of the work should be clearly understood. The young people are given responsibility to mark through the material and to evaluate their competence and performance. To do this well requires the ability:

- to break down the work into sections
- to be aware of problems
- to repeat (not necessarily working full out)
- to refine and assemble to gain proficiency.

This method requires a good movement memory[*] and demands a certain level of competence, attention and responsibility. Weaker young people, left on their own, will not necessarily be accurate enough and teachers will need to observe individual problems so as to be able to give feedback and guidance. To avoid disruption inattentive young people will need to be challenged.

Results may be judged by the progress made by each individual in terms of participation, skill performance and interpretation. Effective self-evaluation will enable the young dancer to translate perceived distinctions in movement quality into sustained improvement.

An extension of this method is for each young person to work with a partner - to observe her/him and give corrections. Examples of this could be:

- a technique exercise
- a section of a folk dance
- a piece of choreography

[*] Obviously movement memory is trained primarily by the simple act of repeating movement material. It can be developed by creating opportunities to recall, copy and repeat movement sequences accurately. The teacher's physical demonstration is further complemented by the use of language to reflect to the class the progressive refinements being sought.

3. Problem solving.

The problem solving process begins with the teacher either posing questions or setting a task to which the young person has to find answers or solve. This is similar to Mosston and Ashworth's 'divergent style' in which, they suggest:

"... the learner is engaged in discovering and producing options within the subject matter. It invites the learner to go beyond the known." Mosston and Ashworth *(Merrill Publishing Co. 1986).*

> *Examples:* How many ways can you find to travel through space with different body parts leading?
>
> Put together a sequence which emphasises contrast in the size and speed of movement.
>
> Use appropriate movement material to create an atmosphere of tension and suspense.

Response to the task is individual and so the outcome is different for everyone. Any decision is acceptable provided the problem is solved. This method encourages individuality and diversity as the task is open-ended.

The young people are involved in decision making - not about reproducing material but about producing options. This approach helps them to understand the process of learning - from the initial enquiry and exploration to the solution and structuring of the subject matter.

Teachers need to provide conditions for a variety of responses to flourish. The atmosphere of the class should foster a learning environment in which individuals feel able to express themselves. The teacher's observational skills will be required to give additional guidance and stimulus when necessary. Further challenge or differentiation of tasks should be considered to ensure that individuals are motivated and are not falling back upon safe and familiar movement material. Tasks can be set for young people as individuals or with others.

4. Collaboration.

This approach invites co-operation in learning rather than encouraging rivalry and competition. It also implies the development of a close relationship with, and tolerance of, others (even if short-lived) and a willingness to share experiences and thoughts with them. In the process of collaborating, those in the class have to develop skills of negotiation and an ability to organise work.

They are also given opportunities to analyse tasks and to arrive, by negotiation, at conclusions. Such relationships enable the fostering of critical, yet positive, attitudes towards the work of others.

Consideration will need to be given to the most appropriate size of a group. Everyone should be encouraged to contribute - not only the strong dominant characters. This is unlikely to happen in groups which are too large. Progress will be assisted if:

a) exploration and forming of movement material has occurred earlier in the lesson so that each person has experience from which to draw and something specific to contribute

b) the group task is clearly structured

c) a time limit is given for the completion of the task.

Young people should be persuaded to work with different individuals in order to extend their movement vocabulary and social skills. The teacher's role is to observe how they are progressing and to intervene only when necessary, by commenting to the class as a whole, or to a particular group.

 # Enhancing Practice

Regardless of the style or strategy employed, the impact of a teacher will be greatly enhanced by attention to characteristics of teaching behaviour e.g. how effective is the **presentation** in terms of clarity of intention, imaginative use of language e.g. **imagery** and **participation.**

Presentation

Even an inexperienced teacher should appear confident and be actively involved. One way in which this might be achieved is through the appropriate use of language and of the voice. The ways in which ideas are communicated, the choice and the use of words, are particularly important. Variations in the tone of voice can encourage, challenge, demand, and praise. If the voice is used expressively, it can vitalise the movement and clarify the quality:

> *Examples:* "Stretch, come on even further ... S–T–R–E–T–C–H!", "Swing and swing ... and **susp**-e-n-**d** .. and ..release".

Voice helps to establish rhythm and the accent of a movement as well as setting the phrasing:

> *Example:* "Travel 2..3.., travel. 2..3.., TURN .., and hold".

Imagery

Imagery can be particularly fruitful when it connects directly with the experience (and if possible the culture) of young people. An appropriate image can be helpful in highlighting correct placement and clarifying bodily response.

> *Example:* "Think of the spine as a string of beads. When you are standing tall with good placement, the beads stretch to their furthest extent with space between the vertebrae. When the spine is relaxed and curled up, the beads fall gently in a loose curve."

Imagery helps a young person to strive even further for a specific movement quality and to feel the embodiment of the image. Imagery can increase and enrich the young person's verbal and movement vocabulary, stimulating creative ideas for exploration and instigating movement responses. Images evoke sensory experiences, stir the imagination, and heighten awareness. They can also illuminate a dance and help to make the movement significant and articulate. Imagery is helpful when exploring the HOW or the QUALITY of movement and can play a special part in increasing communicative and expressive skills.

An image may be used as a stimulus for a dance lesson, but the choice should be carefully considered, e.g. teachers should not ask young people to BE objects or animals, but should draw attention to particular characteristics that would be fruitful to explore in the dance class.

> *Example:*   'bird-like'
> Explore aspects of shape, pathways and locomotion.
> Explore characteristics of claws, wings and focus.

Here are some examples of images that may be helpful in stimulating unusual movement possibilities - and in so doing may enable the young people to explore ideas beyond their existing frameworks of reference.

Between two panes of glass	-	limited two-dimensional use of space
Endless space	-	unlimited use of all the space
Balanced on a tightrope	-	precarious linear pathway
Edge of a precipice	-	balance and suspend
Bottomless chasm	-	focus; look down; endless drop
Footsteps	-	follow someone's pathway; copy
Magnet	-	body parts drawn together
Steam roller	-	flattened to the floor
Vacuum	-	sucked to the walls
Hotplates	-	keep feet off floor; jumps
Elastic and chewing gum	-	stretch out different body parts in different directions
Glue, tar	-	feet stuck to the floor
Cobweb	-	fine movements, reaching, suspended patterns in space
Wading through water	-	resistance
Express train	-	travel very fast; direct pathways
Metronome	-	regular rhythm/s
Pendulum	-	weighty, even swing
Earthquake	-	instability; loss of balance
Lightning	-	unpredictable, erratic movement

Participation

Active participation by teachers is important and they should respond physically when necessary. There may be times when set material is being taught and teachers will want to demonstrate clearly for young people to copy and follow. Demonstration may also be the most appropriate way to give an example of how to achieve a particular skill, for example, doing a 'plié' in preparation for a jump - i.e. aligning and bending knees over toes. It is helpful to use one member of the group to demonstrate good practice. Active participation by a teacher also involves joining in occasionally, moving across and round the room and changing teaching positions.

Joining in and observing have to be delicately balanced. Knowing when to do one or the other comes from recognising the needs of the class. Sometimes individuals or groups, when developing and perfecting material, will need additional help from the teacher. This may involve physical or oral participation by giving ideas and helping to solve problems.

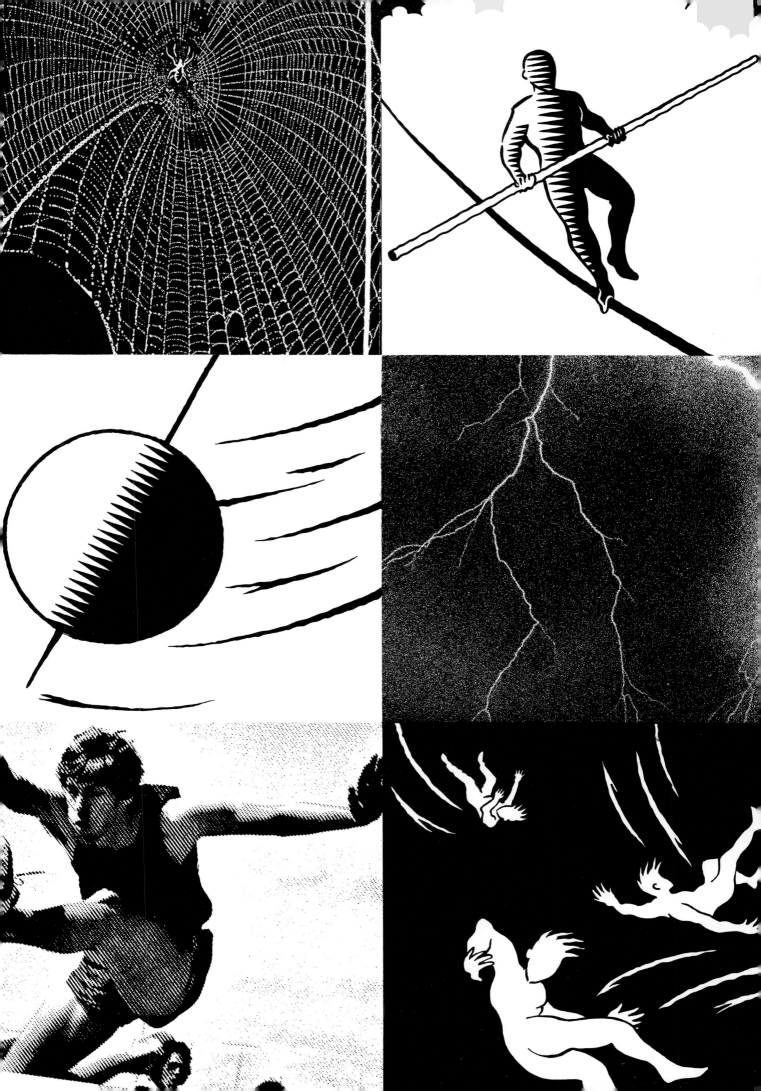

Photo: Adam Eastland Contemporary Dance Trust

Learning to Dance: The Key Processes

Learning to dance involves many different processes, for example:

observing, copying, exploring, improvising, selecting, sharing, collaborating, practising, refining, performing, perfecting, analysing, looking, considering, discussing, reflecting.

Education in dance involves three crucial elements:

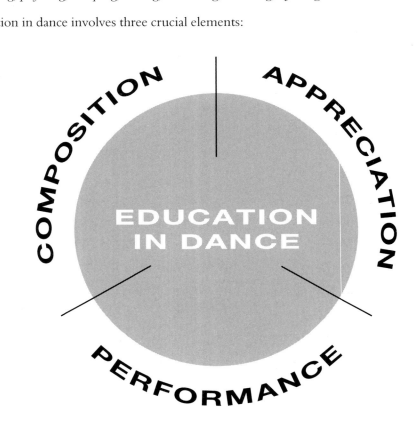

In many lessons, all three elements will come into play. New material can be explored, selected and arranged to form a short composition which can be performed, observed and analysed. It is neither necessary nor desirable that each of the elements - composition, performance, appreciation - should be given equal weighting in every lesson, but they are inextricably linked. Sometimes, however, teachers will want to give attention to one or two elements, e.g.

Composing: Time might need to be spent on *exploring* and *improvising* new material in order to encourage young people not to be predictable and safe in their movement patterns.

Performance/Appreciation: A class might be working toward a finished dance performance for an audience. This could involve *collaborating, practising* and *perfecting* material; and also *discussing* and *reflecting* on its artistic quality and effectiveness.

Appreciation: Young people might be given the opportunity to *observe* videotapes of dance performances. They could be asked to *consider* the movement qualities of a particular style of dance or to *analyse* a choreographic work.

All art activities are concerned with feeling, sensing and perceiving and give opportunities to make connections with the world around us. The creative process in art making is concerned with the desire to communicate ideas, feelings and emotions and through abstraction give them expressive shape, form and intention. The arts in education enable young people to interpret ideas in a given medium. This involves making aesthetic judgements about the choice and selection of material and the form of the composition.

The arts enable us to communicate in a particular way. Music, drama, visual art and dance each have a form of expression and language which is specific to them and distinct. One art form cannot act as a substitute for another. Each offers a different kind of learning, although the processes and procedures might be similar. Dance gives the opportunity to express ourselves with our bodies, the body being the instrument of expression. The ability to be articulate gives us power to communicate and to express ourselves effectively. Expression through dance gives empowerment because it enables a dancer to make a personal statement in a unique way.

"The value of dance is dance. It is a unique and vital communication which needs no further justification, whether professional or educational." Maxine Sheets Johnstone *(Dance Books 1979)*

Engaging Positive Attitudes from Young People
Preparation

Differences in intellectual, emotional and physical development of young people in the middle years is of particular importance to a dance class. Physical maturity might not match up with intellectual or emotional maturity, due to rapid periods of growth - or the reverse. This can lead to insecurity in the dance class, where attention is drawn to the body and a young person may feel physically exposed.

This self-consciousness may manifest itself in certain kinds of behaviour in which the response to dance might be aggressive or there might be a reluctance to participate. Young people may be unwilling to work with someone of the opposite sex, or to touch another person. For this kind of work to be acceptable and 'normal', teachers will need to work hard to establish an atmosphere where young people feel secure, comfortable and value each other.

Teachers will need to be sensitive to those from different ethnic and religious groups. For example, some might be required to adhere to a rigid dress code which might place some restrictions on their movement. They might also have cultural aversions to certain movement patterns. Care in the handling of such issues will be required to ensure that young people from different cultural backgrounds are able to participate fully. Differences should be viewed positively and discussion of them between young people should be encouraged. Cultural diversity should be seen not as restricting but as enriching dance education. Opportunities should be taken to encounter music and dance of different cultures through practical classes, video tapes or live performances.

Practice

Teachers should draw attention to the available working space and to any danger points - for example, fire extinguishers, table corners, etc. Dance is often taught in spaces which are used for a variety of activities and are not always conducive to dance. For the new teacher, a dance class can be particularly daunting - all those young people moving about in a large space! However, it should be apparent that the teacher has an enthusiasm for dance. Certain boundaries concerning how to use space and relate to others should be established to avoid collision and to show respect for personal space.

Clear guidelines should be set up as to the form of the dance class, the expectations of both acceptable behaviour and achievement. The teacher needs to offer a secure environment in which the young people do not feel self-conscious nor exposed and where an atmosphere of respect for the subject and for each other is encouraged. Such a context is necessary if creativity is to flourish and the development of dance is to be realised.

It is important to establish a commitment and seriousness for the work. Use words like

Listen! Look! Stop! Ready! Freeze! Stretch! Hold!

in order to encourage and control.

Active participation should be demanded. This involves a readiness to move - not leaning against the wall or radiators, nor talking to a friend. Emphasise that being ready requires a preparation and concentration of both body *and* mind - not just a lack of movement. **"Stop"** does not mean simply still; it means no movement, no sound, yet being alert. **"Stretch"** means reaching as far as possible, with *everything* stretching and holding the shape. When working on a movement phrase, importance should be given to the beginning and end of the phrase as well as the action. It is a movement statement and should be clear and executed with confidence. The movement should not collapse at the end; ask the young people to visualise the phrase:

This is my beginning, this is how I move and this is how I finish.

Ground rules need to be established when the teacher wishes to draw attention to a particular point:

"Everyone! Stop what you are doing ... and listen."

means exactly that. Each person needs to be still, quiet and attentive.

44

Freeze! Photo: Adam Eastland Contemporary Dance Trust

Teachers should try to keep eye contact with everyone by moving round the room and changing teaching positions. Attention can be gained by changing the way the class is facing or by sending those at the front to the back . This enables different members of the group to be in a more prominent place at different times.

In order to encourage interest and full participation, teachers should aim to include variety and challenge within the tasks. Young people should be urged to extend their movement range and not rely on safe, familiar patterns of movement. The teacher needs to be actively involved in observing individuals by giving praise and encouragement and suggesting ways in which they may achieve a more skilful or expressive result.

Ask questions:

- "Can you reach even higher?"
- "Can you make your shape more angular?"
- "Can you lead more smoothly from the turn into the travelling section?"

Involve the class in decision making. Ask them to offer suggestions regarding the form of the dance and give opportunities to select appropriate music.

Encourage them to have personal integrity for their work; urge them to evaluate positively their work and that of others. Foster interaction between young people and teacher and between members of the class. All work should not automatically be shown. Work demonstrated should be of good quality and should demand a commitment to it by the performers and the audience. Challenge anything less than the best that they can accomplish; give attention to detail and use criticism constructively.

Those sitting out through illness or injury should be given observational tasks to encourage a sense of participation.

Designing the Curriculum

The document <u>Dance in the School Curriculum</u> *(Arts Council 1989)* states that dance contributes to the curriculum in the following ways through:

- artistic and aesthetic education
- cultural education
- personal and social education
- physical education, health and fitness
- cross curricular learning
- prevocational education

All these aspects are important, but some are of particular importance to young people at Key Stage 2 and 3. Young people at this stage are subject to great physical and emotional change and development. As has been discussed earlier this is a period of rapid growth, but the level of development varies with each individual. Young people at this age are often self-consciousness and uncomfortable with their bodies. This lack of confidence can be observed, for example, in awkward posture and embarrassment in relating to members of the opposite sex. Physical and emotional maturity will vary with each individual. These differences can be clearly observed in the dance class.

Dance can be especially helpful in developing co-ordination, strength, stamina and a facility for movement, all of which encourage physical confidence. It can also stimulate interaction and sensitivity with others in developing relationships, which is another area in which they may feel vulnerable.

"The creation of a dance is necessarily connected with individual growth, self realisation and the ability to work well with others ..." Maxine Sheets Johnstone *(Dance Books 1979)*

Since in education we are concerned with development of the whole person, the dance curriculum will need to reflect this. The aim should be the maximum personal development of each individual. We should take account of the needs and interests of all young people and recognise and value individual differences. Each individual is valued and ALL OF THEM CAN DANCE.

The challenge is to take all of the above conditions into account in producing an effective dance curriculum.

The principles of design

When designing the dance curriculum it is important to establish clear *aims* and *objectives*. These will be informed by the *programmes of study* for each Key Stage. The sequence of the curriculum content should be dictated by educational principles. These principles should take account of the *physical, emotional* and *intellectual development* of the young people. The teacher should plan a programme that is *continuous* and *progressive*. This requires long term planning. Work will need to be broken down into suitable units and episodes. It is important that there be logical progression from lesson to lesson and from unit to unit. Opportunities should be given for *development* and *differentiation* within the tasks as well as increasing the degree of *difficulty* and *complexity*. Clear goals and specific intentions should be identified. The choice of material should not be haphazard nor capricious, but should be determined by the application of *valid criteria*.

The above principles should be embraced in delivering the stated achievement levels at Key Stage 2 and 3 as printed below. Following that is an example of how a broad theme can be broken down into units that follow the principles of design.

Key Stage 2: Programmes of study

Pupils should:

- make dances with clear beginnings, middles and ends involving improvising, exploring, selecting and refining content, and sometimes incorporating work from other aspects of the curriculum, in particular music, art and drama

- be given opportunities to increase the range and complexity of body actions, including step patterns and use of body parts

- be guided to enrich their movements by varying shape, size, direction, level, speed, tension and continuity

- in response to a range of stimuli, express feelings, moods and ideas and create simple characters and narratives in movement

- describe and interpret the different elements of a dance.

Key stage 3: Programmes of study

Pupils should:

- be taught how to develop and use appropriate methods of composition, styles and techniques to communicate meanings and ideas

- be guided to create and perform short dances showing sensitivity to the style of accompaniment

- be taught to perform set dances, showing an understanding of style

- be taught to support their own dance compositions with written and/or oral descriptions of their intentions and outcomes

- be taught to describe, analyse and interpret dances recognising stylistic differences, aspects of production and cultural/historical contexts.

case study

Example of design: The Environment

The following is an account of a dance project designed for a group of teenagers on a residential course. It could be adapted and considered as a unit of work of the dance curriculum covering, say, half a term's work for young people in school. It gives opportunity for exploration of a wide range of movement material - and can be seen to cover all aspects described in the programme of study for Key Stage 2 and three of those listed for Key Stage 3.

As well as contributing to the dance curriculum, this should stimulate discussion concerned with broader environmental issues and cross-curricular themes promoted through the National Curriculum such as:

health education ● environment education ● education for citizenship ● personal and social education

Underlying issues may be brought to life in a unique way through dance.

Environment

The project began with an introductory discussion about the meaning of 'environment' which generated lots of images and the practical class which followed explored the most evocative of these images in movement. The broad theme was initially differentiated into three main units:

'Different landscapes' - forests, mountains, desserts . . .
'Environmental disaster' - pollution, oil, nuclear waste, . . . and effects
'Cityscape' - buildings, architecture, urban life . . .

An example lesson follows illustrating the potential and scope of the work.

Lesson

Movement Aims	Action, space, dynamics
Stimulus	Different landscapes

Warm Up

Explore different ways of moving through space using changes of speed, pathways, levels. Images: *stairs, lifts, conveyor belts, express trains, journey to school.* Try combinations of movements.

Movement Exploration and Development

Explore different ways of turning using changes of speed, space, and level. Images: *tornado, whirlpool, spinning top, planets.* Try combining movements.

Explore different ways of balancing, e.g. try balancing on one leg, forward, backward, sideways. Experiment with phrases of movement which switch from balance to off-balance into fall and recovery, e.g. *tightrope, mountain pathway, window ledge.*

Put together a phrase of travel, turn, balance, fall, recover.

Consider how the phrase would adapt to different environments/landscapes:

- in a very narrow confined space - e.g. two-dimensional between two panes of glass
- where there is resistance to movement - e.g. wading through water up to your waist
- where the pathway changes direction, level, height - e.g. pathway through a jungle
- own choice of environment

Appreciation and Evaluation

Show examples of the phrase, using different kinds of environment.
Discuss the changes in movement qualities and dynamics.

Further Development

Working in groups of four or five, build an environment from materials normally found in the dance space, e.g. *benches, mats, tables, chairs, ropes* . . . . . .

Find ways in which the action phrase - travel, turn, balance, fall, recovery - can lead you over/under/around/through the prepared environment. Develop a group dance using individual and unison movement. Subsequent units then build on the range of movement achieved as they develop work on aspects of 'Environmental Disaster', 'Cityscape' and with other possible extensions such as: 'Environmental Adaptation' - lifestyle, fashions, temperature and `Environmental Conservation'- protecting, recycling, restoring.

Evaluating the Lesson

Effective dance teaching involves careful preparation and presentation of material that will stimulate and challenge the young people. It also requires perceptive observation skills.

"Sound teaching stems directly from informed observation." D.E.S. *(H.M.S.O. 1972)*

Such perceptive observation by the teacher draws attention to young people's needs and aspirations, and to the effectiveness of the teacher's skills.

Evaluation of the lesson gives opportunities for the teacher to consider:

- the response of the young people
- the content and presentation of the material

Implicit in the function of teaching is the need to take time to reflect on the effectiveness of teaching practice. The following checklist suggests some ways of self-evaluation.

The Lesson

a)   Were the movement aims clearly established?

b)   Was the warm-up effective?

c)   Did the exploration and development section stimulate creative ideas/imaginative material?

d)   Was there natural progression from one section to the next?

e)   Was the accompaniment suitable?

f)   Were the aims achieved? If not, why not?

Presentation

How effective was the teacher in her/his use of

a) voice and language?

b) demonstration?

c) stimulating imaginative responses?

d) observing and critiquing?

e) organisation skills?

f) time available?

Response

Were the young people stimulated and challenged?

Evaluation of Progress

Progression is the most exciting part of a teacher's work (some would say the most difficult also!). It allows the teacher to move beyond the fragmentary character of any individual lesson and observe the unfolding experience of the young person throughout the course of a whole programme of learning. It provides indicators that assist the teacher to ensure a continuous experience of learning for the young person, but one founded on incremental, successive, planned achievements.

The logic of the Key Stages approach is enabling, and not confining, in that it allows the teacher to take into account the variable speeds at which individuals develop. You may find it rewarding to read the D.E.S. (Welsh Office) <u>Proposals on Physical Education for ages 5 to l6</u> *(H.M.S.O. 1991),* specifically paras. 8.8 to 8.17 with its succinct description of the process of physical development of the young person.

A very clear and helpful description of progression is outlined in para. 8.13 which is worth repeating:

"Pupils generally move from:

- *dependence to independence in learning;*
- *performing given tasks to being able to structure their own;*
- *using given criteria to judge others' performance to developing their own criteria to evaluate their and others' performance;*
- *simple tasks to difficult and complex ones; and*
- *natural movements to skilful/artistic technical performance." (H.M.S.O 1991, op.cit.)*

In a subsequent guidance document on physical education by the National Curriculum Council *(H.M.S.O. 1992)*, progression is described as gradually increasing *difficulty, quality, independence* and *interaction*. Whilst all of this is valuable and directly applicable to teaching dance, there is a need for dance teachers to work with a concept of progression more specifically related to the inherent characteristics of dance development.

Evaluating the progress of an individual in dance should be a continuous process and evaluation should be formative as well as summative. If you recall in the 'Learning to Dance' section three processes were identified: *composing, performing* and *appreciating*. Teachers will need to consider what indicators of progress there might be. They will need to ask such questions as:

- *"What are the young people able to do now that they could not do previously?"*
- *"Does their behaviour reflect changes in their knowledge, skills and attitudes?"*

Teachers will need to identify criteria for progression and these should relate directly to how effective young people are in the areas of **Composition, Performance** and **Appreciation.** Important dimensions are listed below:

Composition
- Has the movement vocabulary improved in range from familiar movement patterns towards more unfamiliar movement?
- Are they able to link movements into meaningful sequences?
- Are they able to make appropriate movement choices with regard to different stimuli and accompaniment?
- Are they able to show increasing awareness of compositional skills?
- Are they able to deal with more complex rhythms?
- Does their work indicate creative and artistic development?

Performance
- Are they able to demonstrate an increased facility for movement, e.g. in terms of clarity and fluidity?
- Does their work show development in physical skills, such as awareness of correct alignment, ability to balance, to jump and turn efficiently?
- Are they able to communicate ideas through movement?
- Do they show an enhanced understanding of performance skills in artistic interpretation?

Appreciation

- Are they able to describe/interpret/analyse/evaluate their own work and that of others?

> In order to illustrate the effective usage of these criteria, the following more detailed example is given using **one** question from **each** of the three areas.

Composition

Objective: 'Ability to demonstrate increasing awareness of composition skills'.

In evaluating the progress of the young person in her/his development of composition skills, the teacher should be able to see the following:

- interpretation of an idea in terms of movement
- movement phrases with clear beginning, middle and end
- use of variety and contrast in the phrases
- development of movement ideas with effective transitions
- more complex works showing awareness of the dance space
- increased sensitivity to the musical accompaniment.

The following sequence of tasks is an example of progression:

a) Make up a dance in response to given stimuli
   For example: Theme - computer games
   Movement content - travelling, turning, jumping, with change of speed and direction

b) Develop phrases of movement which have clear beginnings, middles and ends

c) Work with a partner in a number of ways
   For example: mirroring, copying, contrasting, question and answer

d) Put a phrase together, giving attention to the transitions

e) Introduce contrast and variety to already developed phrases (motif and development) by using changes of time, space, direction, size, etc.

f) Consider different kinds of accompaniment and their effects
   For example: electronic music, words from instructional manual, Brazilian samba.

Performance

Objective: 'Development in physical skills - ability to balance'.

In evaluating the progress of the young person in her/his development of the ability to balance, the teacher should be able to see the following:

- effective use of strength and energy
- control of body weight
- clarity of body shape in space
- efficient use of counterbalance
- clear use of focus.

The teacher will need to give young people a range of movement experiences to help develop these skills.

The following sequence of tasks is an example of progression.

a) How many different ways can you balance on one leg?
b) Try to use different parts of the body to steady the balance
c) Whilst balancing, send energy to all those parts of the body
d) Be strong in your pose
e) Choose a still point in space on which to focus
f) Hold the stillness in a clear body shape
g) How many different ways can you approach a balance? (e.g. from travel, jump, turn)

More complex tasks to do with balance:

h) On how many different parts of the body can you balance?
i) Explore the contrast between moments of balance and off-balance (suspension, fall and recovery)
j) Try this idea (i) with a partner, using holds and body contact (counterbalance, falling and catching).

Balancing on different body parts Ludus Dance Company

Balance with partners Photo: Dee Conway Ludus Dance Company

Appreciation

Objective: 'Ability to describe, interpret, analyse and evaluate dance works'.

In evaluating the progress of the young person in her/his development of appreciation skills, the teacher should be able to identify the following:

- attention to their own work and that of others
- observation with concentration
- ability to describe and analyse

The teacher should provide a number of experiences which enable the young person to develop an ability to articulate, evaluate and reflect upon what s/he sees. These are preliminary stages towards the ability to offer a critical analysis which reveals an understanding and appreciation of values and the worth of the dance concerned.

The following sequence of tasks is an example of progression. These questions should be applied to their own work or that of professional choreographers:

a) Watch, recall and describe (What did you see?)

b) What do you think this dance is about? How does it make you feel?

c) How is the dance put together? (structure and content of the dance)

d) In what ways does it remind you of other dance pieces? (compare and contrast)

e) Make a critical analysis of a dance. (Which part is most effective and why? Is anything missing? What would you expect to happen next?)

Conclusion – Keys to Quality

QUALITY

TEACHING PROCESS
that takes account of
knowledge & skills
teaching & learning methods
the needs of each
individual

TEACHING STYLES & STRATEGIES
that draw on a variety of approaches e.g.
demonstration
self evaluation
problem solving
collaboration

ENHANCING PRACTICE
through
effective presentation
vivid evocative imagery
active participation

LEARNING TO DANCE
the processes involved in
composing
performing
appreciating

ENGAGING POSITIVE ATTITUDES
by encouraging
young people
to have integrity
in what they do

DESIGNING THE CURRICULUM
so that it is
logical
progressive
with clear criteria
for achievement

EVALUATING LESSONS
in such a way that
the teacher can
review what has
been achieved

EVALUATING PROGRESS
using specific criteria for
composition
performance and
appreciation

chapter three

the professional partnership

"It's a long time since I have seen such concentration" Photo: Dee Conway Ludus Dance Company

The Professional Partnership

"I felt all funny inside with enjoyment."
Gary, aged 8

"I'm glad it wasn't one of those teddy bear efforts."
Ben, aged 10

"It was so exciting to see the dancers on stage and then work with them. It made me feel very special."
Lisa, aged 13

Providing young people with access to professional artists and live performances is essential for their understanding, appreciation and enjoyment of dance as an art form. Performances, workshops and educational support material for schools can be a valuable stimulus for learning by bringing the young person into contact with the professional art and artists. For a teacher this stimulus can provide themes and ideas for a term's work in dance and cross-art form projects.

In no other art form but dance is access to live performance so important. Despite recent developments in recording dance, the experience of watching it on film and video is still mediated by recording and transmission. Live performances and work by professional artists in educational settings mean that the experience of dance and its immediate nature are brought into the world - the here and now - of the young person.

"My days at school are memories of blank long days, sitting at a desk trying to make sense of what was being said. Rarely did I feel I was using my imagination or by using the arts as practical study, applying the meanings of knowledge." A Parent

When a dance company enters a school, there is an impact. The strong visual imagery of costumes and sets, the immediacy of live music, the lighting and atmosphere are all powerful stimuli to the imagination of the young people. When the company, such as Ludus, bring with them a programme of workshops, sometimes utilising cross-art forms, the professional partnership with the teacher becomes particularly real. This chapter looks at how such collaboration can feed into and integrate with the most stringent curriculum requirements and is a 'case study' based on the partnership between Ludus Dance Company and teachers during the *Winds of Change* performance tour.

"It was absolutely astonishing as a visual spectacle. I am still coming to terms with it. The school is a better place for having seen it . . . . It is a long time since I have seen such concentration by children over such a sustained period of time." A Head Teacher

From *Winds of Change* performance Photo: Dee Conway Ludus Dance Company

"As a dancer, I find that dancing is the most important thing in my life. When I work with children, I feel I have succeeded if they think that dance is the most important thing for them for an hour."
T.C. Howard, Dancer, Ludus Dance Company

Ludus was formed in 1975 by a group of young performers and teachers in Lancaster. It is Britain's first and foremost Dance in Education company. By performing and teaching in schools, Ludus provides a means for young people to explore issues related to their culture and environment. Each year Ludus devises a new dance theatre production which is strongly issue- or topic-based, age-specific and of direct relevance to the intended audience. Recent programmes have explored, for example, censorship, environmental concerns and conflict. The company is continually developing an ambitious fusion of dance, visual theatre and original music, drawing freely on a variety of cultural styles and forms.

One of their pieces, *Winds of Change* takes the formidable presence of the wind in our lives as the inspiration for three dance pieces devised by different choreographers. The power of the wind evokes a whole range of emotions - great loneliness, great passion, from the first breath of hope to the fear of the most powerful destructive force in nature. It also provides for us startling images from which the choreographers created their dance material and through which young people can explore and learn. Each of the choreographers uses a particular and distinctive style of movement in their work.

Some of these different ways of moving have been used as a basis to develop lesson material in terms of **Movement Aims** for Lessons 1 - 3 respectively.

1. The wind as *breath* - a fundamental source of movement and spirituality in many Eastern cultures
Shobana Jeyasingh - Body shape, body parts, focus

2. The wind as a *force* - exploring the obvious relationship between the movement potential of wind and dance
Scott Clark - Space, body shape

3. The wind in our *psyche* - its effect on our emotions
Louise Richards and Kevin Finnan - Body, weight, relationship

The National Curriculum Working Group on Physical Education for ages 5 - 16 was asked *"to take account of the contribution which physical education could make to learning about other subjects and cross-curricular themes, including in particular expressive arts subjects (including music and drama), health education and personal and social education ....".* *(H.M.S.O. 1992)*

The lesson plans are offered as possible treatments of cross-curricular themes and indicate how dance may be used as a medium to develop issue-based work. Dance lessons might also be designed, for example, to focus upon one or more of the following themes:

technical skill
physical challenge
keeping fit
relaxation
co-operation
communication
multicultural issues
gender issues
enhancement of the imagination
education of the emotions
aesthetic awareness.

Whilst dance can provide opportunities for the development of issue-based work, the primary concern should be the particular contribution made by dance.

lesson plans

The lesson plans which follow address the programmes of study for Key Stages 2 and 3. Additional time will probably be needed to give opportunity for more movement exploration and development of the material. This is particularly the case for younger or less experienced groups. Ideas for progression are given in the 'Further Development' section for each lesson.

The first three lesson plans are given as examples of using cross-curricular themes as **Stimulus** for dance.

Lesson One

Stimulus – Introduction to South Asian Dance

Lesson Two

Stimulus – The Environment

Lesson Three

Stimulus – Conflict and Cooperation

The stimuli for the other lessons are based upon imagery suggested by the theme *Winds of Change.*

Lesson Four

Stimulus – Flying and Falling (one)

Lesson Five

Stimulus – Flying and Falling (two)

Lesson Six

Stimulus – Moods and Unpredictability

NB. Language in the lessons is primarily directed towards young people, for ease of use by the teacher; occasionally additional specific recommendations are inserted to alert the teacher to a point of emphasis or for further development ideas.

lesson ①

Movement Aims
Body shape, body parts and focus

Stimulus
Introduction to South Asian Dance

Accompaniment
Music: Tabla/percussion
Visual Material: Books and pictures of South Asian Dance e.g. <u>Rhythm in Joy: Classical Indian Dance Traditions</u> by L. Samson *(New Delhi: Lustre Press 1989)*

Do not discuss stimulus nor use tabla music until indicated★*. This is to guard against the introduction of preconceived or stereotyped ideas.*

Warm Up

Accompanied by tambour and tambourine. Begin with whole-body activities, e.g. stretching, bending, opening and closing.

Running gently through space; concentration on straight and curved pathways. Develop these pathways into travelling phrases ending with emphasis on the following body parts:

- elbows and knees
- hands and feet
- any of the above
- repeat one of the phrases, adding focus on one body part.

Choose one phrase and repeat beginning and ending with stillness. Copy someone else as accurately as possible.

Movement Exploration and Development

Find a comfortable sitting position from which you can move. Explore the use of hands, e.g. sides, knuckles, finger tips, heel of hand, palms and backs.

Choose three parts and try out ideas. Consider if hands work independently or together, and how they are used in space. Introduce a change of time.

Develop a short sequence which includes a moment of stillness, (teacher should indicate length, e.g. 4 bars of 1 2 3 4). Be sure to include use of focus.

Find a partner and teach each other the sequence and put them together, i.e. a + b.

★ Now introduce tabla music.

Decide on an interesting starting position, not facing each other, but perhaps side by side, one diagonally behind the other etc.

Discuss how the music influenced the work. Look at pictures of South Asian Dance and discuss movement characteristics.

With your partner, choose one or two poses and copy them exactly. Develop a short travelling sequence using the chosen pose(s) including a change of time. What kind of movement does the pose indicate, e.g. linear or turning? Does it suggest a forward, backward or sideways direction?

Begin the dance composition with sitting section, followed by travelling section influenced by poses. Attention will need to be given to transitions from floor to pose, and from pose to travel.

Appreciation and Evaluation

Show work of two or three couples at a time. Direct observation with questions such as:

"How effective were the transitions? What directions were used in the travelling section?" etc.

Return to discussion of South Asian Dance, using books and pictures. Draw attention to the range of dance styles, e.g. Bharata Natyam, Kathak etc..

Further Development

1. Performance and/or workshop by South Asian dancers.
2. Enrich experience through exploration of the dance styles and music of many cultures.

Unnikrishnan Photo: Chris Nash
Pushkala Gopal, Unnikrishnan and Company

Akram Khan Photo: Tricia Scott
Kathak Student 1991

Anjali Photo: Tony Gaston

lesson ❷

Movement Aims	Space and body shape
Stimulus	Environment: confined and free
Accompaniment	Music: *Revolutions* Jean Michel Jarre

Warm Up

Travel through space:

a)   keeping as far away from everyone as possible

b)   keeping as close to everyone as possible without touching.

Explore the space using curved pathways. Use different body parts to initiate the movement. Try to make the movement as continuous as possible.

Explore the space using linear pathways. Change direction sharply when meeting people, walls, etc.

Allow different body parts to lead the movement. Introduce phrases of movement and stillness.

Movement Exploration and Development

Find your own space. Stand tall, being aware of good placement. Explore your personal space using a combination of curved and stretched shapes. Make the movements flow from one to another.

Discuss different environments. When do you feel free and safe, or trapped and confined?

Imagine a confined space, e.g. hole, box, tunnel. Examine its shape and surfaces with different body parts, e.g. back, finger, knee. Hold the movement still in an interesting shape. Develop a phrase which involves three variations of movement and stillness.

Share ideas with a partner. Try to fit together in the moments of stillness like pieces in a jigsaw.

Imagine endless space. Using all the room, develop travelling phrases ending in large, stretched shapes. Involve use of contact with floor and walls.

Try joining up with other people.

In small groups of three or four, compose a dance which shows :

a confined and
a free environment - using any of the material explored, plus your own ideas.

Appreciation and Evaluation

Show the work of a few groups at a time. Discuss which groups used the space particularly effectively.

Further Development

Environmental issues - e.g. pollution, conservation
Rural and urban environments.

Suggestion:

Introduction: Divide group in two. Ask a person from one group to make a shape against the wall which expresses part of a city environment. Ask the rest of the group to add to the shape. Discuss.

Ask the other group to show a rural landscape. Discuss the differences.
Where do they feel more comfortable, and why?

Develop dance material to suggest rural and urban settings.

lesson ③

Movement Aims _____ Body, weight, relationship

Stimulus _____ Conflict and co-operation

Accompaniment _____ Music: *Diva* (original soundtrack).
Vladimir Cosma

Warm Up

Begin with whole-body activities, e.g. stretching and releasing, swinging and giving in to weight movements.

Move through the space.

a) purposefully, confronting anyone you meet

b) hesitatingly, avoiding anyone you meet, no eye contact.

What happens to the body? Do your movements change? e.g. floor pattern, body posture.

Go to your favourite part of the room. Reach out towards someone.

Join up with someone and travel through the space, holding on and taking up:

a) as much space as possible, pulling away from one another

b) as little space as possible - keep very close together

Repeat last (a) and (b) using different holds and levels.

Movement Exploration and Development

Discuss the stimulus. When do we experience conflict or co-operation? How do we show these feelings in the body?

Choose a partner to work with. Explore weight-taking and supporting, e.g. take your partner's weight on your back; with your side; with one body part. Try to make the movement smooth and continuous, taking turns to take weight.

Explore holding and resisting - one partner trying to leave, the other holding her/him back, e.g. use different body parts, different levels, vary the use of time.

With partner, explore shapes (moments of stillness) which show conflict and co-operation.

Compose a dance which includes all or some of the following:

- weight-taking and supporting
- holding and resisting
- moments of stillness and use of travelling to show conflict and co-operation.

Appreciation and Evaluation

Show work, two or three couples at a time. Direct observation with such questions as:

"How many variations of weight-taking did you see? How was the dance resolved?"

Further Development

- Contact improvisation workshop
- Dance lesson using issues as stimulus.

Photo: Adam Eastland Contemporary Dance Trust.

Stimulus: *Winds of Change*

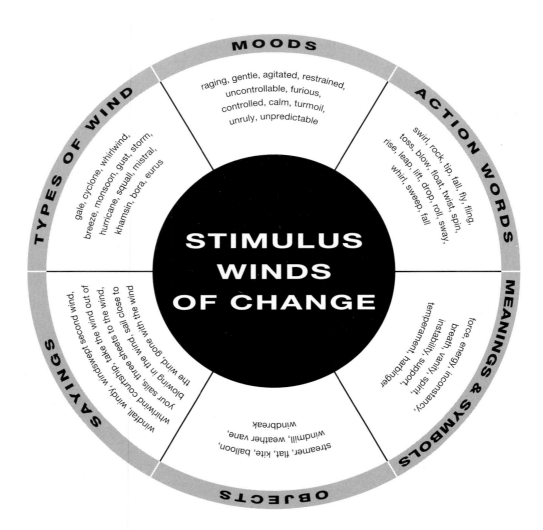

MOODS
raging, gentle, agitated, restrained, uncontrollable, furious, controlled, calm, turmoil, unruly, unpredictable

TYPES OF WIND
gale, cyclone, whirlwind, breeze, monsoon, gust, storm, hurricane, squall, mistral, khamsin, bora, eurus

ACTION WORDS
swirl, rock, tip, fall, fly, fling, toss, blow, float, twist, spin, rise, leap, lift, drop, roll, sway, whirl, sweep, fall

MEANINGS & SYMBOLS
force, energy, inconstancy, instability, vanity, spirit, breath, support, temperament, harbinger

OBJECTS
streamer, flat, kite, balloon, windmill, weather vane, windbreak

SAYINGS
windfall, windy, windswept second wind, whirlwind courtship, take the wind out of your sails, three sheets close to the wind, sails, gone with the wind, blowing in the wind

STIMULUS WINDS OF CHANGE

BURSTING SWIRLING RO
STORMY COOLING BREEZE
ATTER SURGING TURBULEN
EST HURTLING BUFFETING TU
TROLLABLE STILL UNBRIDLED
RAUGHT WAFTING IRREPRES
NED WHIFF GENTLE WHIPPING
BLOWN BUSTING ROARING
ULENCE FLOW TEMPEST BLUST
E QUIET PEACEFUL SMOOTH SOFT
IL LULLING TRANQUIL BUFFE
TING UNCONTROLLABLE STILL U
OOTHING DRAUGHT WAFTING
IBLE RESTRAINED WHIFF GE
ING SMOOTH BLOWN BUSTING
URGING TURBULENCE FLOW
ERY GENTLE QUIET PEACEFUL
HIPPING TURMOIL LULLING
BUFFETING TWISTING
UNBRIDLED GALE SOOTHING D

lesson 4

Movement Aims

Weight and suspension

Stimulus

Winds of Change: flying and falling (one)

Accompaniment

Music: *White Winds* Andreas Vollenweider
Beating of Wings Andrew Poppy

Warm Up

Begin with whole body activities, e.g. lift and drop, and swings with an emphasis on suspension.

Explore the following actions:

travel, fall, roll, stretch.

Put them together in a sequence which repeats (each action to use 10 counts); repeat the same sequence (each action to take 5 counts).

Emphasise the need for continuity and good transitions.

Movement Exploration and Development

With a partner, explore the sensation of falling. Use imagery of a precipice or a ledge, with one partner using her/his weight to support the other, e.g. holding around the waist; one hand; one foot, etc. Change over. Explore different methods of support.

Join up with another couple and explore the sensation of flying. Find ways of supporting one of the group (one body part to remain in contact with the floor). Everyone to have a turn.

Develop a movement phrase of coming together, supporting one of the group, i.e. flying emphasis of lifting and suspension, and changing into falling emphasis on dropping and giving in to weight.

In groups of four, compose a dance which combines the travelling sequence from the warm up and some of the ideas of flying and falling explored. Use the imagery of wind to influence the phrasing of the movement.

Appreciation and Evaluation

Show work of quartets. Discuss how effective the groups were in showing the contrasting movement qualities. What methods of support were used?

Further Development

a) Flying and falling (two) - see Lesson 5

b) Dance lesson using 'Dreaming' as a stimulus. Flying and falling are images which occur in dreams. Other ideas to explore might be running, being chased and coming up against obstacles and barriers.

Photo: Dee Conway Ludus Dance Company: *Winds of Change* performance.

lesson 5

Movement Aims	Body shape, space, impulsive movement
Stimulus	*Winds of Change:* flying and falling (two) Objects affected by wind
Accompaniment	Music: *And Do They Do* Michael Nyman

Warm Up

Begin with whole body activities. Repeat exercises from Lesson 4, based on lift, drop and swings.

Lying on the floor, lift different parts of the body in turn and relax back into the floor. Emphasise the beginning of the phrase i.e. the lifting. Gradually make movements larger and come to standing. Gently give at the knees, catch the body before it falls. Roll up through the body, breastbone leading to another part of the room.

Warm up legs and feet.

Movement Exploration and Development

Look at objects, e.g. kites, newspapers, washing. Discuss their shapes and how they might move on a windy day.

Find different body shapes while lying, sitting, kneeling, standing, reaching. Try different combinations and add travelling, including actions explored in Lesson 4, i.e. roll, fall and add jump.

Choose four favourite combinations. Practise your sequence a number of times, working on clarity of body shape, space and smooth transitions. Repeat the sequence using the imagery of wind as an external force instigating the movement, i.e. use impulsive movement(s) to highlight parts of the phrase.

Repeat the sequence either:

● using the imagery of one of the objects, or

● actually using them in your dance composition

Appreciation and Evaluation

Show work in groups according to choice of objects. Discuss how the sequences are influenced by the nature of the object.

Further Development

Workshops using actual objects, e.g.

- different kinds of clothing

    - for holidays

    - leisure activities

    - work

- different kinds of footwear

    - slippers, wellington boots, high-heeled shoes.

Photo: Dee Conway Ludus Dance Company: *Winds of Change* performance.

lesson 6

Movement Aims

Time, weight, flow

Stimulus

Winds of Change: moods and unpredictability

Accompaniment

Music: *And Do They Do* Michael Nyman
Visual Material: Pictures from newspapers
<u>Manwatching</u> by Desmond Morris
(Triad Granada 1981)

Warm Up

Travel through the space, moving

a)   very quickly

b)   very slowly

c)   with changes of speed.

Travel through the space moving

a)   very lightly

b)   with strength

c)   combining the two.

Choose one particular mood, e.g. angry, sad, happy. Move through space in that manner. Develop phrases which combine changes in time and weight. Now try a contrasting mood. Share your work with a partner. Guess which moods were presented. What kinds of movements were observed?

Notice the changes in *time, weight* and *fluidity of movement.*

Movement Exploration and Development

Look at pictures of people which express different moods and emotions, e.g. elation, anger, despair, etc. Discuss how this affects the body and the way we move.

Explore three contrasting moods, e.g. tentative, furious, happy or restrained, agitated, despondent - use moments of movement and stillness. Put together a phrase combining the chosen three in any order. Movements may be repeated a number of times. Add a movement of surprise, of unpredictability, e.g. sudden change of time, use of weight or space, etc. Be clear about the rhythmical content of the phrase.

Dance Composition

Share material with a partner and devise a dance which involves movements of contrast, harmony and unpredictability.

Appreciation and Evaluation

Show work of some of the most effective dances. Ask the audience to identify the moods observed.

Further Development

- Workshop on voice and movement
- Dance Drama

Photo: Dee Conway Ludus Dance Company: *Winds of Change* performance

chapter
four

dance and other art forms

Dance and Other Art Forms

"All art forms work with abstraction, form, style and intent but the unique essence of each derives from its medium and cannot be readily captured in another medium. Nevertheless, many facets of the one art can be used as stimuli for another." Blom and Chaplin *(Dance Books 1988)*

"Each art form has its own distinctive features, history, body of knowledge, discipline and artistic products. Each also has inherent artistic experience that is different from and complementary to other arts disciplines." National Curriculum Council *(H.M.S.O. August 1991).*

There are a number of ways in which other art forms can stimulate ideas for dance. Much dance work is determined by the choice of music. When dance is performed, lighting, costume and set design as well as sound can be incorporated with the movement.

Ideas from life and the world around us may be explored through any art form. However, the expression of these ideas by the body in motion and stillness, and the intention of the dance work, offers a different interpretation from that experienced in any other art form.

Combined arts projects can be fruitful but require careful planning and collaboration between teachers of the different disciplines. Working together on a common theme can be well worth the effort made.

However, as Margaret Talbot states: *"It is important to concentrate on the integrity of dance across its many forms and its distinctive and peculiar contributions to cross-curricular work should relate back to that integrity."* Talbot *(N.A.T.F.H.E. 1991).*

In this chapter we consider stimuli for dance drawn from the arts taking visual, verbal and aural starting points and give some examples of lesson material.

case study

Contemporary Dance Trust - Rural School Residency Pictorial Case Study

The following photographs were taken by Adam Eastland during a one-week residency, funded by the Lankelly Foundation, at Probus County Primary School, near Truro in Cornwall. The project was led by Contemporary Dance Trust outreach workers Rhian Robbins (dancer and team leader), Gary Hammond (musician) and Maria Godsmark (visual artist). The school had chosen the theme of 'Cats' for the week, as one which 'would appeal to all children and would lend itself to preparatory work in all areas of the curriculum'.

All pupils from Years 1 to 6 took part, everyone having a dance session each day and some 50 taking part in extra art sessions. Preparatory work by teachers had focused primarily on poetry and story writing, and the County Art Adviser had led some particularly successful life drawing classes.

Boys and girls were equally enthusiastic about the dance sessions. Simple actions such as jumping and travelling flowed easily from the theme and provided a starting point for more complex movement sequences.
Photo: Adam Eastland Contemporary Dance Trust.

Movement quality and intention were developed with the help of vivid language and imagery. Different groups used starting points in poetry, narrative, art and music as well as movement.
Photo: Adam Eastland Contemporary Dance Trust.

The children's own work which had begun in the life drawing groups was developed with the visual artist and eventually formed a sculptural backdrop to the dance.
Photo: Adam Eastland Contemporary Dance Trust.

"The Probus Arts Week has provided pupils with a great deal of enrichment across the whole curriculum, and the aesthetic/expressive curriculum in particular."
Peter Kendall, County Adviser for Art.

The professional artist can bring new ideas, perspectives and techniques into the classroom.
Photo: Adam Eastland Contemporary Dance Trust.

Photo: Adam Eastland Contemporary Dance Trust.

Having live accompaniment is not always possible for the class teacher, but does add excitement and stimulus to the dance class.
Photo: Adam Eastland Contemporary Dance Trust.

The week ended with an informal performance which linked the artistic elements of the residency and brought together young people, artists, school staff and audience in a shared social event.
Photo: Adam Eastland Contemporary Dance Trust.

"This was a unique opportunity for children and staff to experience art, dance and music in the company of individuals with a high degree of personal expertise, professional commitment and creative energy.
For a rural primary school, in a very rural county, with limited opportunities to encounter the arts at first hand, the week gave not only an invaluable and enjoyable experience, but the impetus to continue and develop this work in school in the future."
David James, Headteacher

case study

Dance and the Visual Arts

"For many years, the Dance in Education course for post-graduate students at the Laban Centre has included elements which use study of the arts as possible stimuli for dance. This has not only produced imaginative material for dance but also has raised awareness of other art forms.

One particularly exciting occasion was the opportunity to involve students and teachers of dance and art in a workshop and seminar at the Tate Gallery. This collaborative venture was set up with Pat Turner (at that time, Education Officer at the Tate Gallery), Lynda Davis (choreographer) and myself.

The event was unique. We were able to observe a workshop in the North Dureen Gallery in which Lynda Davis showed how she first developed choreographic sketches and then dances, inspired by three art works in the gallery with a group of five dances. After observing the work, she described the choreographic process and we were able to see the structure of the dances develop from the original response to the work of art through choreographic sketches and finished dance works.

This was followed up by an interchange of ideas between students and teachers of dance and art. As a focus for their discussion, they were encouraged to use the following questions as a guide:

How does the painting/dance affect you?

What materials has the artist/choreographer used?

How does s/he present the material?

How does s/he divide up the canvas/space?

Are there similarities/contrasts?

Is it a quiet, calm or a lively, energetic piece?

Does it evoke a mood or feeling?

What are the relationships/groupings?

Discuss the process of a painter/choreographer

Is there a similarity of approach?

Are there words common to both arts?

What are they?

Do they have the same meaning in art and in dance?"

How does the painting affect you?
Photo: Adam Eastland Contemporary Dance Trust.

"A lively discussion followed. Some of the artists expressed concern that the dance interpretation of a work of art might get in the way, diffuse or misinterpret what the original artist's original conception might be. It was felt by some of the group that it was acceptable and usual to write about an art work but less so to dance about it.

Later, students were encouraged to choose a work of art to use as a starting point for dance. The choreographic sketches which they produced were unusual, showing qualities of inventiveness and provided stimulating material for group observation and discussion".

Such kinds of opportunities might be given consideration by teachers. Joint ventures between subject areas and the Art and Dance departments in schools could be attempted. Contact with education departments in galleries and museums might be useful. They may well offer seminars and workshops which would be of value to students of dance. They might also be interested in new initiatives between different art forms.

Dance and Art: Visual starting points

Objects in nature, photographs, drawings, paintings, sculpture and *architecture* can all offer stimuli for dance. Many choreographers have used works of art as inspiration for dance. Isadora Duncan, after visiting the Parthenon, strove to find a way to express the feeling of the human body in relation to the Doric column.

Other, more recent examples are Robert Cohan's *Nymphaeas* influenced by Monet's *Waterlilies* and Richard Alston's *Soda Lake,* the choreographer's response to an abstract sculpture by Nigel Hall. Angelin Preljocaj has choreographed a dance work inspired by Caillebotte's painting *Les Raboteurs.*

Madalena Victorino, a Portuguese choreographer, has produced a number of innovative choreographic works which use the environment in which people live and work as a stimulus and setting for the compositions. One such work *Torrefaccaó* took place in a working coffee factory and used sounds and objects as well as the work processes to inspire the choreography.

Teachers might like to consider the use of unusual spaces for dance in the following ways:

- How the architectural design influences the movement material, e.g. *stairway, narrow corridor, conservatory.*

- How the function and everyday use of the space can lead toward compositional ideas, e.g. *a railway station concourse, a church, a kitchen.*

Design, line, form, space, rhythm, relationships, texture and colour can be used to analyse visual stimuli. One or more of these elements may be utilised in developing material for dance.

If we explore one of them, for example, that of line in relation to dance, the thickness or firmness of line can suggest a feeling of strength or delicacy. A continuous straight line might express sustained directness and a short angular line, rapid change of direction. Line can indicate body shape, air and floor pattern. A number of lines may suggest rhythmical relationships or contrast.

Examination of the texture and colour of a work of art can lead to consideration of how they might influence dynamic changes of movement. An example of how colour may be used in this way is given in Lesson 7.

Visual stimuli may evoke a mood or atmosphere and give a setting or context for dance. They may also be used to suggest a narrative - for example, a dramatic story or historical event.

The following is an example of a dance drama, set in the 1920's and 1930's. Examples of social dance, photographs and costumes of the period could be used as stimuli.

This readily relates to Key Stage 3 Programme of Study, e.g. understanding of dance styles.

A Day at the sea

Music:	Scott Joplin, e.g. 'The Entertainer' (Music from the film 'The Sting')
Movement aims:	Gesture, body parts and relationship
Warm Up:	Work through the body using body parts, taking material from the Charleston, Lindy Hop and other social dances of the period.
Part One:	Working in groups of three or four, develop material for travelling and arrival at the beach. Clothes off and settle down to look at the sea.
Part Two:	Explore swimming, using different strokes; paddling, diving, supporting. Drying off with towels.
Part Three:	Posing for photographs. Finish with a whole group photograph.

Photos: Marion Gough

lesson 7

Movement Aims	Action and dynamics
Stimulus	Colour
Accompaniment	Music: *Colour Symphony* Bliss
	Visual stimuli: Books of paintings, e.g. Matisse, Bonnard, Miró, Kandinsky, Klee

Warm Up

Begin with activities involving the whole body, e.g. swings, stretches. Work on gestural movements. Teach travelling phrases initiated by gesture.

Movement Exploration and Development

Explore the following actions: gesture, travel, balance, swing, suspend, fall. Find new ways to experience each of these actions. Put together an individual phrase using some or all of the actions explored. Find a partner. Show each other your phrase. Discuss their movement content.

Look at pictures from a range of different artists. Discuss how they use colour. How does colour influence the work? What mood does it suggest?

Close your eyes and concentrate on the colour red. How does it make you feel? Return to your phrase. Colour it **red.** Show it to your partner. Discuss the changes in movement quality/dynamics.

Close your eyes and consider the colour blue. What kinds of mood and feelings does it evoke? Return to your phrase. Colour it **blue.** Show your partner. Discuss the changes again in terms of movement qualities/dynamics.

Listen to the *Red* and *Blue* sections of Bliss' *Colour Symphony.* Consider this interpretation of colours.

Return to your original phrase and highlight it with a colour of your own choice.

Appreciation and Evaluation

In groups, show work to rest of class (size of groups to be determined by young people's choice of colour). Look for similarities but bear in mind that we all have very different personal responses to colours.

Further Development

Look at a painting and discuss the artist's use of colour and space, e.g. Kandinsky's *Several Circles* or Miró's *Dragonfly before the Sun.*

Choose a painting and interpret it in terms of movement.

lesson 8

Movement Aims	Body shape, space and relationship
Stimulus	Sculpture/natural objects
Accompaniment	Music: *It's Been Fun* Man Jumping

Warm Up

Travel through the space concentrating on pathways: straight, curved, irregular.

Travel and make a shape: stretched, curved, or twisted. Hold it. Try a combined shape, e.g. part of the body stretched, part curved. Run to meet someone. Touch with different body parts, e.g. elbows, heels, back of the head. Hold the shape.

Exploration and Development

Sit in a circle.

Look at examples of sculpture/natural objects, e.g. pebbles, shells, driftwood. Draw attention to their shape and form when viewed from different angles and levels. Take ideas from the objects and express them by exploring different body shapes. Observe some of the most interesting. Try out a variety of shapes for the following positions: lie, sit, kneel, stand.

Put together a sequence which includes them in any order and with one of them repeated. Share your ideas with a friend. Find a way to combine both examples and include a travelling section and some moments of contact.

Appreciation and Evaluation

Join up with another couple. Show each other your dance and the objects which inspired it. Discuss.

Further Development

- Consider how the work might be shown to the whole group in a way that each pair can place itself as it wishes and where it can be viewed from a variety of angles.

- Reverse the sequence, e.g. begin with the finishing position and work backwards through the sequence to finish with the starting position.

- Starting with natural objects - such as pebbles, driftwood, shells - develop a dance taking the theme of the sea shore.

Music for Dance

How to use music

Music to accompany the dance class can be used in a number of ways. Here are some suggestions:

- To form a background to the dance composition, i.e. to help establish a mood or atmosphere, to highlight a particular movement quality, to heighten a dramatic situation, to act as a boundary in containing the dance.

- Where the structure of the music indicates or dictates the form of the the dance. This gives opportunity to go with or against the music.

- Where different styles of music are used for the same dance, e.g. notice how the quality of movement changes when folk, jazz or pop music are used.

In any event, young people should have the opportunity to listen to the music to be used and to be aware of its particular qualities. It is important that the teacher ensures that the choice of music is complementary to the movement aims. An intimate and thorough knowledge of the music is likely to enhance the quality of the movement.

"The relationship of dance to music is an intimate one. Music, through its pulse and rhythm, provides a driving force and an overall structure. Its influence can be either positive or negative ... The ideal relationship is when dance and music appear as one, mutually supportive, enhancing one another." Blom et al *(Dance Books 1988)*

Knowing music through dancing to it is a different experience from simply listening to it. It involves being able to recall and appreciate with the body as well as the mind. Bodily appreciation is concerned with anticipating the phrasing, changes of rhythm and dynamics, and responding to the spirit of the music. Young people with little experience of working with music may need to imitate it initially. Later they should be encouraged to work towards more adventurous and subtle responses. The intention should be to use music as a supportive device rather than as a direct reflection and to find music that serves rather than dictates the dance. Young people require time to become familiar with the chosen music.

> Don't save music up like a sweet to be given out in the last few minutes of the lesson.

The length of a piece of music to be used in the dance lesson usually needs to be short in order to allow the young people to get to know it well enough so that the dance composition may be repeated a number of times and perfected. The teacher needs to clarify the length of the music to be used, e.g. a section of a piece and to establish the time,

e.g. 8 bars of **1**234, **2**234, **3**234, ...**8**234

> Try to use music of different time signatures - 3/4; 6/8; 5/4; as well as 4/4 - and tempi (slow, fast, leisurely, brisk)

Choosing Music

There is no quick or easy way to find appropriate music for dance classes. Time has to be spent listening to music, building up a collection of useful recordings and making suitable choices.

> Try to get used to having a notebook and jot down the details of any music you hear - on the radio, TV or at a concert - that might be useful. Include information about the movement quality, mood, tempo or impression suggested by the music. It is helpful to place the music under certain headings, such as:
>
> rhythmical, lyrical, dramatic, comic, ethnic/folk.

Tapes and compact discs are more convenient to use than records ever were and a tape/CD player with a digital counter enables the teacher quickly to find the required music. Recordings and equipment used should be of good quality to achieve the best results. Particular attention to this ought to be given when using music for performance. The length of musical works should be considered. Try to find appropriate short works. It is not necessary nor even desirable to use the whole of a lengthy piece of music. A short section of well-edited music may be much more appropriate. Music should not be arbitrarily cut and combining music by different composers should be done with care. The work of composers and musicians should be given due respect, and copyright regulations have to be strictly observed.

Remember that the music used to accompany the dance class will influence the musical taste of the young people. Their musical tastes are often confined to current pop music, some of which can be used effectively in the lesson. However, young people can be introduced to - and begin to appreciate and know - much they might never encounter or otherwise listen to. A wide range of musical choices should be made available involving a variety of styles and cultures and should include some examples which are other than European or North American. The Virgin Directory of World Music and New Sounds are useful publications offering a range of possibilities.

> Look into the possibility of using live musicians to accompany at least an occasional class. You might be able to involve a school group or band or a talented musical student or parent.

Dance and Drama

Stimulus from text, words, sounds.

Text

Sources such as myths, legends, stories, novels, poetry, magazine and newspaper articles are readily available and varied enough to be accessible to young people at different age ranges and can be used as a stimulus to provoke ideas for dance. Stories of other times and cultures can be used to inspire rich movement exploration of ideas. For example, the idea of creation as viewed by different groups and cultures - Native American peoples, Hindus and physicists/cosmologists.

When using text, the dance might follow the form of the narrative (dance drama) for example, a section from J.R.R. Tolkien's The Hobbit *(Harper Collins 1991)*. Another possibility, using literature as a starting point, would be to explore the quality of movement evoked by a text such as Mary Norton's The Borrowers *(Puffin 1952)* - exploring the idea of being very small in a large environment.

Ideas for dance can be inspired by the text of articles in newspapers and magazines, recounting current events and issues. Headlines, sports reports and horoscopes can also be used. All these can lead to broadening a range of movement experiences and providing a heightened appreciation of both the imaginary and the real world.

Poetry

Poetry can be a valuable resource for stimulating ideas for dance.

Japanese poetry such as Haiku and Tanka is *"... concerned with the sudden, surprise effects of metaphoric juxtaposition"* Monaco, R. and Briggs,J. The Logic of Poetry *(McGraw Hill 1974).* They try to express a momentary flash of awareness and an insight into the emotions by a succinct and economic use of poetic language. The reader is required to use her/his imagination and make her/his own associations to complete the meaning of the poem. Each poem can have several layers of meaning. They can be an excellent source for the dance lesson, providing interesting starting points for movement material.

Another way in which poetry might be used could be to explore the movement images of fog which are described in an extract from The Love Song of J. Alfred Prufrock by T.S. Eliot *(Faber and Faber 1974).*

Words

Words can spark off ideas for dance. They can also encourage an interest in language and extend a young person's vocabulary.

Begin by using words which express action. e.g.

sprawl, throw, shrink, swirl, burst, snap, melt, skim, collapse, spring, tremble.

Lesson material could be developed as follows:

a)   Select a number of action words and explore them in movement in a variety of ways
b)   Develop a movement phrase
c)   Repeat the phrase, changing the element of time
d)   Repeat the phrase, changing the use of space
e)   Reverse the order of the phrase.

Qualitative words can be used to colour or to highlight movement material.

For example, the use of words such as *tenuous, bold, expansive, devious, tentative* suggest **how** - the quality with which an action can be performed.

The phrases in the following lists express moods and feelings and can be used to good effect to produce comic and dramatic movement for dance. The lists are not exhaustive.

List One: Familiar sayings using body parts

eyes down	elbow in your way	to be all ears
in the palm of my hand	led by the nose	all fingers and thumbs
head in the clouds	back to back	shoulder to shoulder
straight from the heart	spineless	weak-kneed
shake a leg	without a leg to stand on	best foot forward

List Two: Phrases which express moods and situations

balanced on a tight-rope	pulled in all directions	poised on a knife edge
fired with anger	seized with panic	clutching at straws
bowled over with surprise	knocked for six	doubled up in pain
filled with love	overcome with grief	wallowing in self-pity
walking on air	frozen with fear	high as a kite

Sounds

Sounds can be made with the voice, e.g. *sing, hum, moan, whoop, hiss, shout.*

They can be made with different body parts and contact with different surfaces, e.g. *clap, click, stamp, slap, rub.*

They can be used to stimulate ideas for dance with either the sound initiating the movement or the movement initiating the sound. These ideas may be explored as solo, partner or group work tasks. For example:

Solo: Develop a dance with an A B form, with the A phrase starting from the sound and the B phrase from the movement

Duo: Develop a question and answer dance using a combination of voice and sound

Groups: In groups, devise an unaccompanied dance which concentrates on changes of level and time. Show each in turn to the rest of the class who first observe and then, acting as an orchestra, accompany the work with sounds. A sound score could be developed.

It should be noted, however, that when using words or sounds to accompany dance some people find the experience inhibiting, others as an opportunity to let rip.

It is necessary to give sufficient time to explore ideas in sound, as one would in movement. Work needs to be carefully structured as this not only gives security, but also helps to keep the sounds under control.

lesson 9

Movement Aims

Action and dynamics

Stimulus

Haiku,
Kite like a soul,
Dancing,
Journeying,
Fallen to earth,
Kubonta

Accompaniment

Music: Tambour. Japanese Flute music
Visual Material: Pictures of birds and kites

Introduction/Warm Up

Begin with whole body activities - bending and stretching, reaching leading into travelling, and then travelling and changing levels.

Exploration and Development

Read the poem two or three times. Discuss the imagery. Draw attention to the development of the poem in terms of movement material, i.e. the actions, space pattern and phrasing as well as the emotional response it evokes.

Experience practically some of the following:

rising, lifting, flying, travelling and falling, e.g. lifting - lie relaxed on the floor, lift a limb. Be aware of the tension pulling the muscles to give the lift. Let go and relax.

Try different limbs, upper torso, hips etc. Stand, give at the knees, catch the body before it falls, rise again. Roll up through the spine until breastbone leads into space.

Begin to develop phrases of movement selected from exploration. Introduce imagery of the wind as an external force to influence the dynamics of the phrase, concentrating in particular on time and flow.

Show your dance to a friend. Consider how you can both keep your sequence intact but combine your work as a duet.

Appreciation and Evaluation

Show two or three couples at a time. Look for dynamic changes of time and flow.

Further Development

- Using the same solo material work with a partner, one taking the part of the kite, the other person holding the strings.

- In groups choose one person's phrase developed in Lesson 9. Everyone learn it and perform it as a flock of birds i.e. following the leader's movement and pathway through space. Each person has a turn as leader.

- Explore other examples of Haiku. Perhaps young people could be encouraged to write their own examples. A cross-curriculum project with the English Department perhaps.

- Look for other examples of poetry to stimulate ideas for dance.

lesson ⑩

Movement Aims
Gesture and focus

Stimulus
Everyday gestural movement

Accompaniment
Music: *Amusing Ourselves to Death*
La Bouche

Introduction/Warm Up

Travel through the space moving towards and away from each other. Now add surrounding each other. Continue travelling through the space, acknowledging others when you meet them. Observe some examples.

Discuss gestures used in greeting. Consider formal and informal, social, children and adults, male and female and cultural uses of gesture in this context.

Exploration and Development

Explore a number of different gestures used in greeting. Develop a phrase of 12 counts, using three different gestures and include travelling, turning and use of focus.

Teach a sequence which includes a variety of greetings gestures. e.g.

Wave and step to the right .... 2 counts
Nod head and step to the left .... 2 counts
Step forward and raise both hands in salute .... 4 counts
Step back on left to medieval bow .... 2 counts
Hands and feet together into Asian bow .... 2 counts

Add own phrase .... 4 counts

Change the movement of the sequence in three ways:
● by making some of the movement very small
● by making some of the movement very large
● by embellishing some parts.

Appreciation and Evaluation

Show the work of half of the class at a time. Decide who each person will observe. Ask them to look for the use of *minimal, maximal* and *embellished* movement and to consider the effectiveness of the use of focus. Discuss.

Further Development

Continue with more gestural movement:

- Combine with a partner to develop a conversation in dance using gesture. Select from the following feelings:

anger, amazement, disgust, amusement, disbelief, boredom, surprise.

- Choose an everyday activity, e.g.

washing up, brushing hair, making a sandwich.

Develop a movement phrase; repeat it exactly. Show it to a friend. Guess each other's activity.

Return to your phrase and *enlarge, diminish* and *elaborate* some of the movements. Show your friend the changes you have made.

chapter five

resources for dance

Resources for Dance

Dance teachers may feel rather isolated in the sense of having no other colleague who can directly relate to their particular professional needs. Therefore, it is important for them to be aware of any available supportive dance network. There are a number of individuals, associations and dance companies, who can be approached to give help and advice in terms of materials and resources for teaching and professional development.

Contacts

Some of the following, in the teacher's local area, might prove useful:

- Advisory Teacher for Dance (or equivalent post) in the LEA
- Community Dance Worker/Animateur
- National Dance Agency
- Dance department in local institutions of Further or Higher Education
- Regional Arts Board Dance Officer
- Regional Dance Councils
- Leisure Services Officer
- Education officers attached to arts organisations, e.g. dance company, theatre, art gallery, museum
- Choreographers
- Musicians
- Other art form advisers/practitioners

Such people might be able to help in terms of the provision of: help for teachers in planning their dance curriculum; classes and workshops for young people or teachers; the creation of choreography and/or music for a dance work; collaborative ventures with other art practitioners; workshops in local galleries, museums, etc. to stimulate ideas for dance; funding and resourcing dance initiatives; a venue where dance works can be shared and performed.

In some areas, you may find Youth Services and Sports Development/Action Sport are working in partnership with LEAs to support dance activities.

Publications and resource material

(For further details see Bibliography)

Teachers will need to consider ways to build a stock of resources within their schools to support dance. These will include magazines, articles, books, videotapes, audiotapes and instruments.

The National Resource Centre for Dance (NRCD) offers valuable help in the way of videotape materials, resource packs, information lists, etc. as well as the publication <u>What's Afoot?</u>

The National Dance Teacher Association (NDTA) publication, <u>Dance Matters</u>, is particularly helpful in discussing current issues in dance education, materials for dance and reviews of new books and other resource materials, as well as giving regional news.

Dance and the Child International (DaCi), UK Chapter, publishes conference papers and a journal - <u>Focus on Education</u> - which offer a wide range of articles about dance education.

A number of LEAs have produced resource materials for dance. One particularly comprehensive document - <u>Dance Curriculum Guidelines 5 - 18 years</u> - was produced by *Staffordshire County Council Education Committee* in 1985. This appears to have been a collaborative venture by a number of teachers. Readers of this book might consider undertaking a similar initiative in their areas.

<u>Dance Theatre Journal</u> produced by the *Laban Centre* makes an excellent contribution to dance criticism and research.

<u>On the Move - Directory 1</u> An *Arts Council and Sports Council* initiative lists dance and movement activities for young people.

<u>Dance in Schools</u> *(Arts Council 1993)* is a valuable free publication which complements non-statutory guidance on dance in the National Curriculum.

Music

The use of music for dance was considered in Chapter Four. There are a number of musicians who have produced tapes of music, specifically for dance. Teachers should consult with the local advisory teacher or community dance worker who ought to be able to help locate them.

Videotapes

Videotapes of young people's work may be used to enable them to evaluate their own individual work as well as that of others. Since many young people rarely have the chance to see a range of live dance performances by professionals, videotapes of dance could be considered to assist this purpose. Tapes of dance works can be used to introduce young people to a wider perspective of dance styles and give them the opportunity to observe and evaluate the works of different choreographers.

Teachers may consider using videotapes of dance work to develop lesson material. Young people might be asked, after observing a dance, to discuss and analyze the movement material and style used by the choreographer, e.g.

Ballet Rambert's *Sergeant Early's Dream,* choreographed by Christopher Bruce.

> Contrast the men's quartet (folk-style with emphasis on stepping and body parts) with the men's trio (movement concerned with weight-taking and overbalancing).

Opportunities could be given for the class to explore these ideas practically.

The **National Resource Centre for Dance** produces and distributes a number of dance videotapes including support material for GCSE and A/AS Level Dance. Many dance companies produce videotapes of their work for use in schools and colleges although union agreements might restrict their ability to provide such recordings. The **Video Place** provides a comprehensive video service, including the opportunity to view a large number of dance performances recorded at The Place Theatre.

Professional Development

Teachers may feel the need for additional training and assistance in certain aspects of the dance curriculum. The **Laban Centre Education Unit** is able to offer this kind of support by visiting schools and giving practical classes and workshops. **London Contemporary Dance Theatre's Education Department** offers a range of education programmes and resources for primary, secondary and special schools.

In order that individual teacher's concerns are addressed, it might be desirable for them to combine with others to consider joint ventures. For example, workshops and a performance by a professional dance group could be shared by a number of schools. This would considerably reduce the financial costs. Some teachers might also act as a pressure group to encourage support in their area for particular kinds of assistance with professional development.

The **National Dance Teachers' Association** holds regular conferences throughout the country which focus on important issues in Dance Education. Some recent examples include: *Gender Issues, Dance and the Gifted Student, Dance in a Multicultural Society, Dance and Special Needs Students.* It also provides a forum for dance teachers to discuss in-service needs.

Dance and the Child International also holds regular conferences in this country. Recent themes include 'Careers in Dance' and 'Young People with Special Needs'. Every fourth year an international conference is held to bring together dance educators. The last conference was held in 1990 at the University of Utah, USA. The next one is scheduled to take place in Sydney, Australia in 1994.

Summer schools

A number of associations and institutions - for example, the **Laban Centre for Movement and Dance**, the **London Contemporary Dance School,** the **Rambert Dance Company** and the **Laban Guild** - offer summer schools, which give opportunity for dance teachers to practise, extend and deepen their knowledge of dance.

Links with professional dance

The following are some dance companies which have education units:

Kokuma	Green Candle
Scottish Ballet - Steps Out	Shobana Jeyasingh Dance Company
Phoenix	Ludus
Rambert	Adzido
Diversions	English National Ballet
London Contemporary Dance Theatre	Northern Ballet Theatre
The Royal Ballet	Birmingham Royal Ballet

They offer a range of services, which include workshops, performances and resource material. Information about these companies (and others) and what they provide can be found in the *Arts Council's* <u>Dance Pack (1992)</u>. This comprehensive document gives detailed information regarding how to work with dance companies - from the initial planning to final evaluation. Another publication by the *Arts Council,* <u>Dance in Schools: Partnerships in Practice</u> gives examples of authorities *"who have developed dynamic partnerships with dance artists, companies and organisations"*. This focuses upon five LEAs whose support for the subject has encouraged a range of interesting initiatives in dance education.

Regional Arts Boards will have details of small to middle-scale companies with education initiatives.

conclusion

Good teachers come in a variety of styles, temperaments and personalities. It is the teacher more than the method that affects our interest in learning. We can all remember one or two teachers who have left a lasting impression, someone who introduced us to new ways of thinking and awakened our interest, enjoyment and appreciation. Good teaching demands more than knowledge and skills. It rests on the ability to communicate passion and conviction, curiosity and enthusiasm as well as expertise. The teacher needs to be able to command attention and influence behaviour - teaching young people not what to think but how to think; convincing others of the value of dance for both girls and boys.

For dance to be truly valued, it needs to be visible. This will involve showing aspects of the work not only within the school to other young people and staff but also to larger audiences of parents and the general public. The use of non-traditional dance spaces might need to be considered in order to reach a wider audience.

In the rapidly changing world of education, teachers should consider new partnerships and collaborations to enrich the dance curriculum as well as to give new perspectives. Links with other schools, community dance workers, professional companies, musicians etc. will be fruitful for all concerned and will help compensate for the poor resourcing that dance has traditionally received.

The social significance of dance cannot be overestimated. The range and diversity of dance forms young people may encounter offer a rich resource for our culture. Dance is particularly well placed to contribute to cultural education and to help us to understand who we are and the environment in which we live.

Dance enables us to communicate and to give expression to our thoughts and feelings in a unique way. As such, dance has a significant role to play in education. It gives opportunity - through being in touch with oneself - to relate experiences from the dance class with daily life. The task of the teacher is to provide a stimulating environment in which it is possible for young people to be creative, imaginative and to respond with enthusiasm to challenges.

bibliography

Arts Council	1991	Dance in Schools; Partnership into Practice	Arts Council
Arts Council	1992	The Dance Pack	Arts Council
Arts Council	1993	Dance in Schools	Arts Council
Blom, L.A. & Chaplin, L.T.	1982	The Intimate Act of Choreography	Univ. of Pittsburgh Press
Blom, L.A. & Chaplin, L.T.	1988	The Moment of Movement. Dance Improvisation	Dance Books
CDET/NATFHE/ NDTA/SCODHE	1989	Dance in the School Curriculum	
Curl, G. (Ed)	1991	Dance Section. Collected Conference Papers Vol 5	N.A.T.F.H.E.
D.E.S.	1972	Movement: Physical Education in the Primary Years	H.M.S.O.
D.E.S. (Welsh Office)	1991	Physical Education for ages 5 - 16	H.M.S.O.
D.E.S.	1992	Physical Education in the National Curriculum	H.M.S.O.
D.F.E.	1992	Physical Education for ages 5 to 16	H.M.S.O.
Davies, S.	1992	On the Move, Directory 1	Arts Council
Desai, A.	1992	The Village by the Sea	Puffin
Eliot, T.S.	1974	Collected Poems	Faber and Faber
Fraleigh, S.H.	1987	Dance and the Lived Body	Univ. of Pittsburg Press
Garaudy, R.	1973	Danser Sa Vie	Paris: Editions du Seuil
Monaco, R. & Briggs, J.	1974	The Logic of Poetry	McGraw Hill
Morris, D.	1981	Manwatching: a Field Guide to Human Behaviour	Triad Granada
Norton, M.	1952	The Borrowers	Puffin
Samson, L.	1987	Rhythm in Joy: Classical Indian Dance Traditions	New Delhi: Lustre Press
Schaefer, J.	1990	New Sounds	Virgin Books
Sheets Johnstone, M.	1979	The Phenomenology of Dance	Dance Books
Shreeves, R.	1982	Children Dancing: a practical approach to dance in the primary school	Ward Lock Educational
Staffordshire C.C.	1985	Dance Curriculum Guidelines 5-18 years	Staffordshire C.C.
Sweeney, P.	1991	Directory of World Music	Virgin Books
Tolkien, J.R.R.	1991	The Hobbit	Harper Collins

Some further references

Abbs, P. (Ed.)	1987	Living Powers: The Arts in Education	Falmer
Brinson, P.	1991	Dance as Education: Towards a National Dance Culture	Falmer
Gulbenkian Foundation	1980	Dance Education and Training in Britain	Calouste Gulbenkian Foundation
Gulbenkian Foundation	1982	The Arts in Schools; Principles, Practice and Provision	Calouste Gulbenkian Foundation
Lowden, M.	1989	Dancing to Learn	Falmer
Harlow, M. & Rolfe, L.	1993	Let's Dance	B.B.C. Educational Publishing
Mosston, M & Ashworth, S.	1986	Teaching Physical Education	Merrill Publishing Co.